MELISSA O\

FROM
WORRY
TO
WONDER

A CATHOLIC GUIDE TO FINDING
PEACE THROUGH SCRIPTURE

ASCENSION

West Chester, Pennsylvania

Ascension
PO Box 1990
West Chester, PA 19380
1-800-376-0520
ascensionpress.com

Cover design by Rosemary Strohm
Printed in the United States of America
21 22 23 24 25 5 4 3 2 1
ISBN 978-1-954881-06-8

This book is dedicated to my four beautiful, brave, faithful, and kind daughters—Emma, Lilly, May, and Daisy.

Though they grew up in Washington, DC, through the 9/11 attack on the Pentagon, anthrax scares, mystery shooters, riots, urban unrest, and human instability,
they always kept their cool and learned early on to trust God and dwell in only what is "twue, no-bell, wight, purr, lubly, and admire-able." Thank you, girls, for living your lives well—for choosing faith, hope, and love.

And to my beloved husband, Dale Overmyer, faithful, strong, smart, kind, and cool as a cucumber. He is God's gift to me.

*Who is like you, O L*ORD*, among the gods?*
Who is like you, majestic in holiness,
terrible in glorious deeds, doing wonders?

–Exodus 15:11

CONTENTS

"We know that in everything God works for good with those who love him."
(Romans 8:28)

"Present your bodies as a living sacrifice, holy and acceptable to God."
(Romans 12:1)

"Be transformed by the renewal of your mind."
(Romans 12:2)

"I can do all things in him who strengthens me."
(Philippians 4:13)

"Cast all your anxieties on him, for he cares about you."
(1 Peter 5:7)

FOREWORD

Life is made up of many choices! Where you live and work, your choice of a spouse, and how you raise your children are all important parts of your life that spring from a decision-making process.

While the more visible and concrete aspects of life seem to rise to the top when it comes to allocating mental energy, it is the decisions that are made deep within the soul that often make the biggest difference. Whether good or bad, informed or ignorant, wise or foolish, decisions are made moment by moment like the beating of the human heart.

Knowing that life demands many decisions, we should turn our attention to the source of our decision making. Whom will we trust, how will our thoughts be influenced, and where will we find wisdom to navigate the crossroads of life in an age of independence, individualism, and self-mastery?

The answer is the Author of life itself, the Creator of the universe, and the One who is the Way, the Truth and the Life, Jesus Christ! If we could choose one person to walk with, consult with, confide in and emulate, we simply could not choose better than the second Person of the Trinity, Jesus of Nazareth.

The good news is that we can walk with him today, just as the apostles walked with him two thousand years ago. In fact, even before any of us entertained the thought of following him, he had already chosen us. Walking with the Lord as a disciple is about being chosen to share in the divine life of the Trinity, now and forever. Being chosen as a disciple is an invitation to his love letters, the Word of God. This in itself is big enough to fill our hearts and minds, but to realize that Jesus calls us "friends" should fill our hearts with overwhelming joy and a sense of certitude about life.

In *From Worry to Wonder*, Melissa Overmyer will share with you her insight as a disciple of Jesus and how that relationship influences her daily decisions. Isn't this what we are really looking for? The beautiful thing is that Jesus does not simply offer suggestions; he offers relationship and, within that relationship, a wealth of love, wisdom, and adventure.

There is a marvelous dance between God and his Bride, the Church, that takes place in the midst of everyday living. At first it may seem a bit awkward and foreign, but after some practice the moves come easier, and a joy begins to rise within the heart as we feel the thrill of moving in harmony with God.

The apostle St. Paul was very aware of the human effort that went into serving God, and at the same time he was aware of the power of God working within him to accomplish the will of God in the world. The revelation that changed everything for Paul was the understanding that it was the grace of God within him that fueled his hard work. He said, "But by the grace of God I am what I am, and his grace toward me was not in vain. On the contrary, I worked harder than any of them, though it was not I, but the grace of God which is with me" (1 Corinthians 15:10)

Those who observed Paul may have concluded that he was a very wise, gifted, and tenacious individual, but Paul knew that it was God's wisdom, Word, and power that propelled him to victory. He told the Philippians, "For God is at work in you, both to will and to work for his good pleasure" (Philippians 2:13).

As you read this book, I pray that your relationship with Sacred Scripture will be your source of strength when worry tries to dominate your thoughts and that wonder will be the fruit of your daily dance with God.

–Jeff Cavins

STARTING OUT

There is an important reason that this book has found its way into your hands. If you are ready to go from worry to wonder, you will find this book a trustworthy guide. Author Melissa Overmyer provides unique insights and powerful Scripture passages that flow with the healing grace of God. She equips you with time-tested truths from the richness of our Catholic Faith that will lead you to greater freedom from pessimistic thoughts and worried feelings.

The Lord is the great healer, the worker of miracles, a faithful friend. Surely Jesus, who worked so many miracles described in the Bible, is still working miracles in the hearts, minds, bodies, and souls of his people today. The tools in this book will give you an opportunity to meet with the Lord, strengthen yourself with beautiful passages from his Word, and learn to trade in needless worry for a powerful trust in his love and goodness. The keys in this book will open doors to greater peace if you dare to use them.

Joan of Arc declared, "All battles are first won or lost in the mind." In my work as a Catholic therapist, my clients and I frequently discuss how thoughts influence mood, which then influences behavior. For example, if I choose to focus on the thought that some people have been unkind to me, that can lead to feeling rejected, which can lead to the unhelpful behavior of isolating. The truth is that I do have a choice about the pessimistic or optimistic thoughts I focus on. If I choose to focus or even obsess on things that haven't gone well, then I can sink into self-pity over the disappointments from the past and can drown in debilitating fears for the future.

There is another option.

When a pessimistic thought drops into my mind, I can ask the Lord, "What do you want me to learn from this experience?" Believe me, the Lord is eager to answer this question. He is magnificently equipped to teach me important lessons from every tragedy and triumph that I encounter. This crucial learning builds confidence that the Lord truly can bring good out of any circumstance that I choose to turn over to him. That knowledge and that experience that God can bring good out of any difficulty inevitably gives me great peace and courage.

You are on the winning team with a mighty God who urges, "Cast your cares on him for he cares for you." As you ponder these pages, you will gain fresh tools and insights about how to win this battle in the mind. Your heart will be lifted in prayer to the One who knows all and redeems all. You will be invited to meditate on powerful Scripture verses and store them in your heart. You will learn how to joyfully live out Padre Pio's injunction, "Pray, hope, and don't worry."

And whatever you do ... please make the time to follow the daily journaling exercise in the back of the book for forty days, which will train your mind to focus on what is good, noble, and true. While this book is not intended as a substitute for those who seek counseling for anxiety, the brief daily journaling exercise has great merit. If you have been asking God for deliverance from the worries that have been plaguing you, this book will be extremely helpful. This is the season to grow in confidence and courage. It is time to trade in worry for wonder.

–Christine Fauci Wittman, MA, LPC

A NOTE TO THE READER

We have had many "What?!" moments in our family. Most recently, while we were on vacation last year, a neighbor called to tell us our house had been vandalized and then set ablaze by an arsonist.

By God's grace we have had just as many "Wow!" moments. When I say "Wow," I mean moments of awe when someone says, "Wow! How did God do *that*?" "Wow! God *is* a wonder-worker!" Or "Wow! He really *did* hear my cry and answer my prayers!" These are the moments when we go from worry to wonder.

Because he has been so faithful—throughout history and to me personally—I now fully expect our awesome and good God to answer my prayers in ways that he sees are best for me, to work everything together for good, and to be my answer to life's problems, big or small.

He can do the same for you.

We lost our home and all our material possessions in that fire, but the peace we have found since then is tangible. Why? Because it is from God. The gifts of the Church—God's truth in Scripture, the grace that flows through the sacraments, the prayer practices tested over thousands of years—outweigh anything this world can throw at us. Our Faith and its teachings anchor us in something greater than what this world has to offer.

One of our biggest "Wow!" moments occurred just after the fire, when we looked back and saw the way God had orchestrated events so that our family and pets were safe and no life was lost. My daughter had been house-sitting while my husband and I were away, but our dog had introduced a tenacious outbreak of fleas into our home. To clear the way for the exterminator, my daughter left with our whole menagerie of pets to stay with friends—and that is when the arsonist struck. A few days earlier or later and things could have been gravely different.

How can I not trust a God who did *that*?

God tells us over and over again in Scripture what to do with our worries: take them to him. As you read this book, please practice the steps, mark up your Bible, and trust him. Every time you turn to Scripture and trust the God who reveals himself there, you will be amazed by his grace.

If you are troubled by anxiety or more serious fears, please seek the advice of a mental health professional or other qualified health provider. Do not disregard professional advice or delay seeking it because of something you read here. I am not a doctor, and I am not proposing that this book be used as your only source of help if you are in need of professional support via a counselor, psychiatrist, therapist, or medication. My hope is that this book will be just one of the many ways God brings you to wholeness, happiness, and peace.

By the grace of God, no matter what comes your way, may you too go from worry to wonder, living fully every moment of every hour of every day as you place your life in God's loving and very capable hands.

–Melissa Overmyer

INTRODUCTION

FROM "WHAT?!" TO "WOW!": LEARNING TO GO FROM WORRY TO WONDER

A few years ago, while on fall break from school, our adventurous daughter Lilly headed to the California coast to meet a friend, celebrate her twentieth birthday, and do some surfing. One afternoon, she paddled out alone into the cold Pacific waters on her surfboard. As she waited for just the right wave, a huge swell arose and several enormous waves came in, one right after the other, pitching her over and driving her headlong into a sandbar below the water's surface. Each time she tried to come up for breath, she was thrown back under and tossed about by subsequent waves.

Miraculously, her adrenaline pumping, she was able to orient herself upward, grab quick gulps of air, find her board, and paddle the hundreds of yards back to shore. But once there, she realized that something was horribly wrong. She signaled for the lifeguards and was immediately placed on a backboard and taken by ambulance to the hospital.

The bad news was that she had suffered unusual and nasty breaks in her neck vertebrae, she had a very severe concussion due to head trauma, and she was in intense pain. The good news was she was alive! Her spinal cord was intact, her body was able to function, the swelling and pain could be treated, and the delicate bones in her neck would mend. But it would be a painful and slow process.

When bad things happen, we often get overwhelmed by them, like the waves that held my daughter under. We go over the details again and again in our minds, giving them the ability to tumble, toss, and hold us captive under a sea of worry. But we too must learn to orient ourselves upward, take life-giving gulps of air, stay afloat, and head to safety!

Scripture guides us, showing us just how to do this. It asks us to shift our focus away from the problem, from being held under, and instead gaze upward to the Answer, to entrust everything to God's care and then rejoice. Yes, we are to rejoice! Rejoicing gives us our life-giving gulps of oxygen. It is not something we do based on our circumstances—it's not that if things are good, we rejoice, and if not, then we don't. No, Scripture states that we are to "rejoice in the Lord *always*" (Philippians 4:4, emphasis added). Rejoicing shows God how much we love him and trust his sovereignty and worthiness to be praised. It enkindles faith in our hearts, reminding us of what an awesome God we belong to. But we can only truly rejoice always when we have first understood who God really is and who we are, acknowledging his strength and our helplessness without him.

Once we have entrusted ourselves to him, Scripture asks us to keep rejoicing and stay afloat in his light. This takes practice. We are to guide our thoughts continually to what is good and "worthy of praise" (Philippians 4:8). We keep giving him our cares, relying on him, acting in him, courageously standing firm in our faith as we ride the seas of life.

But how do we actually do this?

That's what this book is about.

TRUSTING GOD

I come from a long line of worriers. When my father was a baby, his mother would tie one end of a string around his ankle and the other end around hers for fear he would be kidnapped as they slept. His father was a worrier too. My dad inherited their worry-driven mindset, and so did I.

On good days I believed we were just cautious people, good planners, prepared for the worst. But no one can be fully prepared all the time. On bad days I was worn out with worry but believed there was nothing I could do about it.

Then I had the chance to study the Word of God with wise and beloved teachers who showed me that the powerful truths in Scripture are meant for everybody, everywhere, forever. God, as Scripture reveals him to us, is truly the answer to the deepest yearnings of our hearts. Over time, as I began to practice these truths and trust God's promises, my life was transformed. When I practiced what I knew to be true, I was literally set free from constant nagging worries—and for the first time in years I started getting a good night's sleep.

In the days and weeks after Lilly's accident, I used the tools in my spiritual tool kit whenever I started to feel wobbly. Many times each day, I turned to the promises in Sacred Scripture and prayed, giving God one by one the worries that filled my motherly heart. I fought the temptation to let my mind wander and refused to dwell on the "what ifs" of the future and the "if onlys" of the past. I rejoiced in him.

I write this book to share with you what I discovered in Sacred Scripture. It has brought me great peace. By God's grace, he used his Holy Word, the sacraments, and the teachings and practices of the Church to bring me daily from worry to wonder.

The verses and the practices you'll learn on the following pages have helped me through my own "What?!" moments many times now. Instead of looking inward at my problems and worrying, I now look to God, my Answer, and I wonder, "Heavenly Father, Worker of Wonders, how are you and I going to solve this problem together? How are you going to bring good out of this situation as you promise in your Word? What would you like me to learn from this? How, by your grace, can I use this suffering for your good purposes and greater glory?"[1]

And I expect and eagerly await good things.

We never want to limit God. He is an awesome God and can act with power. In my experience, if we pray boldly, staking our claim on his love, his promises, and the protection of his Word, we will receive big answers—in the big events as well as the daily struggles of our lives.

God answered our prayers for our daughter. As promised, he brought good things out of not-so-good circumstances. I was able to spend much one-on-one time with my daughter and love her as I had never had the opportunity to do before. We both came to appreciate the small things, the tender mercies we received each day. We were able to pray, laugh, and cry together. As we sought the Lord, keeping our eyes on him in hopeful expectation, little by little he turned our "What?!" into "Wow!" Lilly made a record recovery and headed back to school that same year to begin again.

LEARNING AND LIVING TRUTH

In John 8:32, Jesus himself states, "You will know the truth, and the truth will make you free."

Jesus longs for us to be set free, to become fully alive by living the truth. But first, we have to learn what the *truth* is. We all must learn the truth because sadly, if we do not, we can fall prey to the alluring yet misguiding voices in our culture or, worse, the Enemy of our souls, who loves to fill our minds with worry and negative thinking. We must train ourselves to recognize truth and structure our lives around it.

Thankfully, the Word of God and the teachings of the Church show us what truth is and how to apply it in our daily lives. And believe me, it works when we follow it: the truth *does* set us free. At the same time, it can be difficult to change our daily habits to live in accord with the truth—impossible, actually, without God's grace.

But praise be to God, he gives us all the grace we need—because anything God asks us to do he enables us to do by literally dwelling in us. This is the wonder of our life in him. Through the presence of his life-giving Holy Spirit, he strengthens us, gives us courage, and gives us abilities beyond our own human capacity. God's Holy Word is his instruction manual for making life work. So as we read it and continually surrender ourselves to him—embracing the gifts he has given to us through the Church and the sacraments, asking him to fill us and fulfill his truth in our lives—we can confidently trust that when he asks us to do something, he also gives us the ability to do it.

And it is all to his glory. St. Irenaeus of Lyons is quoted as writing, "The glory of God is man fully alive."[2] When we cooperate with God's grace, allowing the Holy Spirit to flow through us freely and powerfully, we become "fully alive."

We do our part, and he does his.

My favorite example of this—and the inspiration for this book—is the story of Moses. When the children of Israel were fleeing Pharaoh and his six hundred charioteers, Moses cried out to God for help. God told Moses he only needed to keep the people moving forward, raise his staff, and stretch out his hand; he himself, the Lord God, would do the rest. With the Egyptian army in hot pursuit, here is what happened:

> Then Moses stretched out his hand over the sea; and the LORD drove the sea back by a strong east wind all night, and made the sea dry

land, and the waters were divided. And the sons of Israel went into the midst of the sea on dry ground, the waters being a wall to them on their right hand and on their left. (Exodus 14:21-22)

Moses simply cooperated with God. In an act of faith, he obeyed and did what was humanly possible: he raised his staff over the sea and kept the people moving forward. God did what was *not* humanly possible: he parted the sea with a strong east wind, turning the seabed into dry ground. The lesson? We do our part by God's grace, and God, who is always true to his Word, will do his part. And we try not to get the two parts confused!

I have seen this played out again and again in my own life. God will ask me to do something I think is impossible, and he makes it possible. On a personal level, for instance, it happened when I trusted him each day with my daughter's recovery. On a professional level, there was the time we felt God nudging us at Something Greater Ministries to rent space in downtown Washington, DC, for several weeks to do evangelism and outreach to young adults working in the city. Week after week we were to feed dinner to everyone who came there to explore their Catholic Faith through the Alpha Catholic program that we ran in partnership with the Archdiocese of Washington. We had zero budget to make it happen. Lo and behold, God came through! He provided the funds, the speakers, the team, the food, and—miracles of miracles—the magnificent Shakespeare theater, of all places! I just had to cooperate with his grace and, in an act of faith and obedience, say yes. I had to be willing to do what I could do, and he did all the rest. He supplied the graces needed. He always does.

To be set free for whatever God is asking of me, in the big events of life and in daily living, I wake up and work through what I now call my "Worry-to-Wonder Checklist," basically my check-in with God (see the checklist at the beginning of Part I of this book and A Worry-to-Wonder Checklist to Go at the beginning of Part III). That's what this book is about. In the following pages, we will use the checklist to explore God's promises in detail, and you can use the journal pages at the back to practice putting the checklist to work.

I pray that as you learn the promises and protections God gives us in Holy Scripture and the fullness of divine revelation communicated to us through his holy Church, your relationship with him will grow and he will give you a firm foundation on which to stand.

The longer I walk with the Lord, the more I trust him and am aware of his goodness. I pray that as you read this book he will use it to rekindle in you a childlike faith in him. I also pray that, by his grace, your worries will change to wonder at the sheer goodness of our Lord!

PART I

THE WORRY-TO-WONDER CHECKLIST

THE WORRY-TO-WONDER CHECKLIST

☐ **Refresh your spirit:** Offer yourself to the Lord every morning.

☐ **Plug into the power source:** Know who God is and what he can do.

☐ **Get understanding:** Know who you are and what you can do.

☐ **Be set free:** Cast your cares on the Lord.

☐ **Look up!** Rejoice and be grateful.

☐ **Stay in the light:** Guide your thoughts to what is good.

☐ **Act in God's strength:** Courageously stand firm.

CHAPTER ONE

REFRESH YOUR SPIRIT: OFFER YOURSELF TO THE LORD EVERY MORNING

I appeal to you therefore, brethren, by the mercies of God, to present your bodies as a living sacrifice, holy and acceptable to God, which is your spiritual worship.

–Romans 12:1

The first thing we are encouraged to do every day, not only by St. Paul but by the Church, is called the morning offering. And it is easy to do when we know how much we are loved by God our heavenly Father. It is almost impossible to do if we do not.

In earthly relationships, we cannot fully offer ourselves to someone we do not trust. The same is true in the spiritual world. That is why knowing that you are personally loved by God as his beloved child—and that you can trust in his love for you—changes everything.

We must let that truth sink in. Sit with it for a minute. Soak in his light and his love. Say out loud, "I am a beloved child of God," and let your heart and mind hear it.

Oh, what we won't do for our earthly "beloveds"—the lengths we will go to show them how fervently we love them. God the Father feels exactly the same way about each of us. As we come to know and trust his love, our morning offering will roll right off our tongues when we wake each day:

Here I am, Lord. Fill me with your Spirit.

I like this short offering and also the long one that you will find at the end of this chapter, but you might have another you like better. It is not so much the words we say as the attitude and openness of our hearts that matter.

To borrow a word from St. Thérèse of Lisieux, we can call this offering of ourselves each day to the Lord "abandonment." St. Thérèse wrote, "Abandonment alone brings me / Into your arms, O Jesus."[3]

Do you know the story of St. Thérèse and her "little way"? She was convinced that God wanted her to be a saint, as he does for all of us. But she also knew that she could never get there on her own. She knew about a newfangled contraption called an "elevator." As she contemplated this marvelous invention, she realized that it was just what she needed to get to heaven. She wrote,

> We live in the age of inventions now, and the wealthy no longer have to take the trouble to climb the stairs; they take an elevator. That is what I must find, *an elevator* to take me straight up to Jesus, because I am too little to climb the steep stairway of perfection.[4]

Thérèse found the "lift" for which she was searching: "*Your arms, My Jesus, are the elevator* which will take me up to Heaven."[5] But there was one condition: Rather than growing up, she was to remain little. She was to accept her powerlessness and have boundless trust in his divine mercy.

St. Paul also speaks of "abandonment," only he uses different words— he asks us to offer ourselves to God as a *living sacrifice*. What does this mean? It means the same as "abandonment," to trust in God's boundless mercy alone. It means we offer him all that we are. We die to self, to our own ways, plans, and desires, in order to please God, worship him, and be united to him.

We need to do this every day. We need to renew our self-offering to God *daily*, because the problem with a *living* sacrifice is that it is always crawling off the altar.

THE GIFT OF THE HOLY SPIRIT

As we abandon ourselves to him and empty ourselves out to worship, love, and adore him, he fills us up and brings us to himself. He does not leave us desolate to struggle on our own (see John 14:18). Instead, he gives us *his very own Spirit*, which enables us to walk the Christian (Christlike) life. He is endless mercy.

Ponder this: we have God's very own Spirit living in us.

What does it mean to have God's very own Spirit? St. Paul writes to the Galatians, "It is no longer I who live, but Christ who lives in me; and the life I now live in the flesh I live by faith in the Son of God, who loved me and gave himself for me" (Galatians 2:20).

St. Paul is saying that Christ lives in and through us. He animates our lives with his life. He gives us strength and power and love that we cannot muster on our own. This life is *supernatural*, "above the natural"—we are God's and he is ours. We are one. And that is amazing news! That is how we are to live this life: by abandoning ourselves to him so that we may live a life pleasing to him, because he is living it in and through us. St. Paul states, "Do you not know that your body is a temple of the Holy Spirit within you, which you have from God? You are not your own" (1 Corinthians 6:19).

Holy Scripture states and the Church teaches that we receive the Holy Spirit initially at Baptism: "Peter said to them, 'Repent, and be baptized every one of you in the name of Jesus Christ for the forgiveness of your sins; and you shall receive the gift of the Holy Spirit'" (Acts 2:38). Therefore, if you are a baptized Christian, you have this power in a very special way already within you. St. John Paul II stated, "Do not be afraid. Open wide the doors for Christ."[6] We are to live the relationship we have with Christ in a deeper way by asking that our hearts and minds be opened wide and filled again and again with his life-giving Spirit.

Jesus himself prayed for us to receive the Holy Spirit: "And I will ask the Father, and he will give you another Counselor, to be with you for ever, even the Spirit of truth, whom the world cannot receive, because it neither sees him nor knows him; you know him, for he dwells with you, and will be in you. I will not leave you desolate; I will come to you" (John 14:16-18). Therefore, we are never alone!

In praying for myself and for others to be filled with the Holy Spirit, I have seen that the Holy Spirit brings an amazing assurance of being deeply loved by God, and a supernatural peace accompanies that. He also brings true freedom: "Now the Lord is the Spirit, and where the Spirit of the Lord is, there is freedom" (2 Corinthians 3:17).

The freedom he brings is tangible liberation from everything that is *not* of God—and that means healing in the places where we are stuck, release from the things we cannot seem to overcome by our own willpower. These are what Scripture calls "the desires of the flesh," our earthly, sinful nature (see Galatians 5:16). This healing liberation occasionally comes all at once; more often it comes slowly over time. But it is always accompanied by the assurance of God's love and by what the *Catechism of the Catholic Church* calls the fruits of the Spirit (CCC 1832).

I have struggled with many things in my life, but by the grace of God, each day that I abandon myself to him and walk with him throughout the day, I find true freedom and healing in Christ by the power of the Holy Spirit.

THE FRUITS OF THE SPIRIT

The way that God does this is so delightful! Through his Holy Spirit, God gives us just what we need to combat our unhealthy habit or attachment so that we are not trying to free ourselves in our *own* strength. By God's grace, as we *choose* to practice virtue—"habitual and firm disposition[s] to do the good" (CCC 1803)—in little ways every day, we grow stronger and experience greater life-giving freedom. And before too long, by God's grace and the strengthening of our "virtue muscles," we are able to do things that before we would have thought impossible.

St. Paul names the fruits of the Holy Spirit that help to enable us "to do the good," to live a strong, virtuous, and happy life. They are "love, joy, peace, patience, kindness, goodness, faithfulness, gentleness, self-control" (Galatians 5:22-23), and Church tradition adds generosity, modesty, and chastity (CCC 1832). Wow! Sign me up! Who does not want these? But wait—there's more!

Beyond the wonderfully liberating freedom and fantastic fruit of our faith that come from the Holy Spirit, we are "sealed" by him, the way a signet ring makes a seal in wax. In this way we know that we belong to God and God to us. St. Paul writes, "In him you also, who have heard the word of truth, the gospel of your salvation, and have believed in him, were sealed with the promised Holy Spirit, who is the guarantee of our inheritance until we acquire possession of it, to the praise of his glory" (Ephesians 1:13-14).

To experience this freedom, offer yourself daily to God, abandon yourself to him in faith, and ask that by his grace and mercy you may be filled with his very presence—his life-giving, virtue-enabling, powerful-beyond-your-own-human-strength Holy Spirit.

GROW STRONG IN GOD'S WORD

Now we can see why it is so beneficial to ask God to fill us with his Spirit each day. When we invite the Holy Spirit in, we are enabled to live the Christlike life. The Holy Spirit gives us the gift of himself so that we know that we are God's chosen and beloved children. Look up these verses and pray with them as you offer yourself each morning to the Lord:

- "I will not leave you desolate; I will come to you" (John 14:18).

- "If we live by the Spirit, let us also walk by the Spirit" (Galatians 5:25).

- "In him we live and move and have our being" (Acts 17:28).

- "All who are led by the Spirit of God are sons of God. For you did not receive the spirit of slavery to fall back into fear, but you have received the spirit of sonship. When we cry, 'Abba! Father!' it is the Spirit himself bearing witness with our spirit that we are children of God" (Romans 8:14-16).

PRAYER

This is a beautiful prayer of self-offering by Pedro de la Cruz.[7]

Lord, I offer you all of me, all that I am and all that I am not. I offer you every good decision and every regrettable mistake, every great accomplishment and every missed opportunity, every divinely inspired gift and every unapplied talent, every success and every miserable failure.

I offer you all joy and all heartache, every kindness and every bitterness to be forgotten, every twinkle in my eye and every tear flowing down my cheek, every great love and each lost or irrecoverable act of charity.

I offer you every quiet reflective moment and all of the unneeded chaos around me, all things holy and good in me and all things in need of greater purification.

I give you every joyful memory and every bitter foul pain, each future moment and every missed opportunity to love, every kind act and each regrettable harsh word, all meekness and humility within me and every misplaced prideful thought, every virtue and every weak vice, every laugh and all misery mixed with weeping.

I give you every healthy breath and every weakness of mind and body, every attempt at chastity and every unworthy lustful thought, every restful repose and every anxious sleepless night.

O Lord, you can have all of me, the beauty that you've deposited deep within me and the emptiness of my sinful faults. I love you and am yours completely. Amen.

CHAPTER TWO

PLUG INTO THE POWER SOURCE: KNOW WHO GOD IS AND WHAT HE CAN DO

Do not be conformed to this world but be transformed by the renewal of your mind, that you may prove what is the will of God, what is good and acceptable and perfect.

–Romans 12:2

When we are worried, we need to replace with God's truth any lies whispered into our hearts and minds by the Enemy of our souls, and we need to enlighten our ignorant thinking with faith-based understanding. We can do this in many ways but most importantly by learning who God is and what he can do. Discovering this then allows us to get an accurate picture of who we are, beloved children of the King of kings. It lets us see what we can do, empowered by his grace and Holy Spirit, as we will investigate in the next chapter.

What we are about to explore can be life changing.

We all know that our thinking affects our emotions, and emotions can affect our actions. So if we want to change, we must begin by changing our thinking. If our minds are filled with negative thoughts and images about God or ourselves (or both), we can easily get tangled up in a web of discouragement. Instead, we must seek the truth about God and ourselves as revealed in his Holy Word and the teachings of the Church.

WHO GOD IS

Listen again to Jesus' promise: "You will know the truth, and the truth will make you free" (John 8:32).

We begin by looking to God. The very act of beholding him changes us: "We all, with unveiled face, beholding the glory of the Lord, are being changed into his likeness from one degree of glory to another; for this comes from the Lord who is the Spirit" (2 Corinthians 3:18).

Do you know who God is?

God is love.

Memorize these words and tattoo them on your heart.

Do you know how things were between God and us in the beginning? The first chapter of Genesis tells us that Adam and Eve were blessed by God and had carefree joy in his presence. They trusted and relied on him completely. The trouble started in Genesis 3, when the Serpent deceived Eve and tempted her to doubt God's goodness and his love for her.

The Serpent began by asking a question that contained a cunning lie:

> Now the serpent was more subtle than any other wild creature that the LORD God had made. He said to the woman, "Did God say, 'You shall not eat of any tree of the garden'?" (Genesis 3:1)

The Serpent twisted God's words. God had not forbidden the fruit from *any* tree, just the fruit from *one* tree. The Serpent overstated what God had forbidden. Then he drew Eve's attention to the *one* thing that was forbidden and lied outright about why God forbade it (see Genesis 2:17). The Serpent said, "God knows that when you eat of it your eyes will be opened, and you will be like God, knowing good and evil" (Genesis 3:5).

Thus he led Eve to believe that *God did not have her best interests in mind* and was *withholding something good from her.* He led her to think that if God loved her, he would not have forbidden the fruit from that tree.

If the Enemy of our souls has the opportunity, he will do the same today. He will try to get us to question who God is—to doubt that he is our all-wise, all-powerful, loving Father—and doubt that God's ways are best for us. He will get us to look at our *circumstances*, the things we find troublesome or difficult, and he will whisper in our ears, "Would an all-powerful God who loves you do *that*? Withhold *that*? Cause *that*? Let *that* happen?" As soon as he gets our attention, he plants every seed of doubt he can.

This is why we need to know the truth about God. As we study his Word and grow more confident in our faith, we will see how God's love permeates every aspect of our *entire lives*. We must ask him daily to open our hearts, our minds, and our eyes to him, to renew our minds in the truth of who he is and of his love for us.

GROW STRONG IN GOD'S WORD

Do you want to be truly free? If so, seek the truth of who God is. Here are some powerful verses to remind us of who he is: He is our loving Father, merciful and good, faithful and trustworthy. And he is all-wise, a mighty warrior, and the all-powerful King:

- "Pray then like this: Our Father ..." (Matthew 6:9).

- "We know and believe the love God has for us. God is love" (1 John 4:16).

- "O the depth of the riches and wisdom and knowledge of God! How unsearchable are his judgments and how inscrutable his ways! 'For who has known the mind of the Lord, or who has been his counselor?' 'Or who has given a gift to him that he might be repaid?' For from him and through him and to him are all things. To him be glory for ever. Amen" (Romans 11: 33-36).

- "Who is the King of glory? The LORD, strong and mighty, the LORD, mighty in battle!" (Psalm 24:8).

WHAT GOD CAN DO

We know that God is our all-wise, all-powerful, loving Father.

Is anything too hard for him? Let's uncover the truth and be set free from any uncertainty.

God is the "King of kings and Lord of lords" (Revelation 19:16). He is our "Holy God, Holy Mighty One, Holy Immortal One," as we pray in the Divine Mercy Chaplet.

We live in a world where doubt reigns supreme and where stories of tragedy fill our newspapers. We don't often hear much about the miraculous, but it happens. God is very much alive and active, and if we look, we will see his hand at work in people's lives every day.

God in his merciful, infinite goodness protects and keeps each of us every day. He is actively present in our daily lives. Each breath we take is his gift to us.

Is *anything* too hard for God?

No! Remember how God parted the Red Sea so the Israelites could cross on dry land? How he gave them manna to eat in the desert? And think of the people Jesus healed and raised from the dead! In his passion, death, and resurrection, Jesus conquered sin and death! (See Ephesians 4:9 and Acts 2:24). As we learn more and more about the Lord, we come to trust that *nothing* is beyond the reach of his authority, his lordship, and his redeeming hand. Nothing at all. And that is what gives us hope.

Reading stories about how God uses his miraculous power for the good of his children strengthens our faith and increases our hope. The story of Daniel's friends (in the book of Daniel, chapter 3) is a particular favorite of mine.

The children of Israel often found themselves in less-than-ideal circumstances. Hananiah, Azariah, and Mishael were three good Jewish boys who were taken into captivity in Babylon, where they were known as Shadrach, Meshach, and Abednego. As part of their "assimilation process," they were made to serve in the court of Nebuchadnezzar, the Babylonian king. There they were ordered to bow down to a large golden statue and worship it whenever a signal was given. But they were faithful, trusting followers of the Most High God, and they refused. So the king had them thrown into a fiery furnace.

These young men knew that God, if he chose, could deliver them from the hand of the king and from the white-hot fire. But what is even more wonderful is this: they trusted God's loving plan for them so deeply that *even if he did not deliver them*, they would not turn away from their faith in him. Listen to their words in answer to King Nebuchadnezzar:

> "There is no need for us to defend ourselves before you in this matter. If our God, whom we serve, can save us from the white-hot furnace and from your hands, O king, may he save us! But even if he will not, you should know, O king, that we will not serve your god or worship the golden statue which you set up." (Daniel 3:16-18, NAB)

When they refused to bow down, they were thrown into the furnace. But when the king looked into the furnace, he saw not three men but four! And the fourth looked like "a son of God" (Daniel 3:92, NAB). When the young men were released from the furnace, not a hair on their heads had been harmed, and their clothes did not even smell of smoke.

Amazing! God can do all things! He is *all-powerful*. We may not personally see God's hand move in such spectacular ways, but we can have faith that he is at work on our behalf, even in hidden ways, behind the scenes in our own lives. May we, like Daniel's friends, have the kind of faith that knows we can trust him in everything. He is with us and has the power to get us through, no matter the severity of the trial or suffering. In him we can place our full trust.

GROW STRONG IN GOD'S WORD

Bolster your faith and ask God to move on your behalf. Here are some verses to pray with, to remind you that God provides safe refuge for his children and works for our good. He can accomplish what seems impossible to us and will give us strength:

- "O taste and see that the LORD is good! Blessed is the man who takes refuge in him!" (Psalm 34:8).

- "We know that in everything God works for good with those who love him, who are called according to his purpose" (Romans 8:28).

- "Jesus looked at them and said to them, 'With men this is impossible, but with God all things are possible'" (Matthew 19:26).

- "Yours, O LORD, is the greatness, and the power, and the glory, and the victory, and the majesty; for all that is in the heavens and in the earth is yours; yours is the kingdom, O LORD, and you are exalted as head above all. Both riches and honor come from you, and you rule over all. In your hand are power and might; and in your hand it is to make great and to give strength to all" (1 Chronicles 29:11-12).

PRAYER

Dear God, I know that you are real and that you are here.
I know that you see me. I know that you hear me. And I know
that you love me, and that is why I can confidently place my
trust in you today. I also know that you are my loving Father,
all-wise and all-powerful, and that nothing is too hard for you.
I know that nothing is beyond your reach or capability. You are
God—the Awesome One! God—the Powerful One! And God—
the Holy One! Please increase my capacity to trust even more
fully in who you are and what you can and will do on my behalf.
Please help me to notice and be grateful for the big and small
ways in which you act for my good in all things. I place myself
fully in your loving hands today. Amen.

CHAPTER THREE

GET UNDERSTANDING:
KNOW WHO YOU ARE AND WHAT YOU CAN DO

I can do all things in him who strengthens me.

– Philippians 4:13

More good news and hope! Knowing who you are is the next step in letting the truth free you from worry.

WHO YOU ARE

Do you know who you are?

If the Enemy can make you doubt who you are—or better (for him), *whose* you are—he has won the battle. It is important to learn the powerful truth of *who you are* so you can take a stand against the Enemy's lies.

I am God's beloved child. And by his grace, I am chosen, redeemed, and capable of holiness and victory!

You know that God is your Father. But do you know that you are his beloved child? And do you know that God loves you simply because … he loves you?

He loved you before he created the world. He made you in his own image. You are his own child, his "baby"! He doesn't love you because of what you do, how successful you are, how much money you make, or even how holy you are. He loves you because you are *his*.

We cannot earn this love. It is what the Church calls *grace*, which means "unmerited favor."

The *Catechism* says this about grace:

> Our justification comes from the grace of God. Grace is *favor*, the *free and undeserved help* that God gives us to respond to his call to become children of God, adoptive sons, partakers of the divine nature and of eternal life. (CCC 1996)

He loves you so much that before he created the world, even knowing your capacity for sin, he decided to make you anyway. Think about it: He knew before creating you that in order for you to be redeemed and share in his blessed life, it would cost him his earthly life. And he did it anyway. This is an extraordinary love!

Our Creator is also our *abba*, which means "daddy." As his beloved children, we have incredible access to him.

There is a story I once heard in a homily that illustrates this beautifully. After Abraham Lincoln entered the White House, he began the practice of opening the doors and granting an audience to anyone who wished to see and speak to him. Soon, though, the corridors were so crowded that the White House staff limited his open-door policy to only a few days per week. This made getting in to see the president very difficult.

Here is where the story picks up:

> Following the Civil War, a dejected Confederate soldier was sitting outside the grounds of the White House. A young boy approached him and inquired why he was so sad. The soldier related how he had

repeatedly tried to see President Lincoln to tell him he was unjustly deprived of certain lands in the South following the war. On each occasion, as he attempted to enter the White House, the guards crossed their bayoneted guns in front of the door and turned him away. The boy motioned to the soldier to follow him. When they approached the guarded entrance, the soldiers came to attention, stepped back, and opened the door for the boy. He proceeded to the library where the president was resting and introduced the soldier to his father. The boy was Tad Lincoln. The soldier had gained an "access" (audience) with the president through the president's son.[8]

Just as Tad Lincoln had access to his dad, we always have access to our Father as well. Nothing can separate us from him. God made you out of his love for you, and he redeemed you out of his love for you. You are God's beloved child, and by his grace, you are chosen, redeemed, and capable of holiness and victory.

You see, when you know whose child you are, everything changes. You can let go of worries more easily because you know your heavenly Father has your back. You can walk in faith and confidence knowing that you are, in fact, God's beloved child. And you can rest in the assurance that your heavenly Father hears the cares you voice in your prayers and he receives them in hands that are infinitely stronger and more capable than your own.

GROW STRONG IN GOD'S WORD

May we never tire of contemplating who—and whose!—we are. We are God's beloved children, redeemed by him and so deeply loved by him that he gave his life for us. And he will provide what we need for victory over the struggles we face!

We can renew our minds in the truth with these powerful verses:

- "See what love the Father has given us, that we should be called children of God; and so we are" (1 John 3:1).

- "In him we have redemption through his blood, the forgiveness of our trespasses, according to the riches of his grace" (Ephesians 1:7).

- "For God so loved the world that he gave his only-begotten Son, that whoever believes in him should not perish but have eternal life" (John 3:16).

- "Thanks be to God, who gives us the victory through our Lord Jesus Christ. Therefore, my beloved brethren, be steadfast, immovable, always abounding in the work of the Lord, knowing that in the Lord your labor is not in vain" (1 Corinthians 15:57-58).

WHAT YOU CAN DO

We have just explored *whose* we are. Now let's discover what we, by God's grace, can *do*. Here is what St. Paul says:

"I can do all things in him who strengthens me" (Philippians 4:13).

Notice that Paul does not say, "I can do it all by myself." It is through the Lord that we can do what we need to do. The Lord gives us strength.

We are meant to keep our eyes on him and be filled with his strength.

But no matter who you are, great or small, the Enemy of our souls wants you to keep your eyes on *yourself* and *off of Christ*. As long as you are thinking about yourself, the Enemy can tempt you and get you off track.

You can think either *too much* or *too little* of yourself, but neither is what the Lord intends. As one successful author writes, true humility is "not thinking less of ourselves but thinking of ourselves *less*."[9]

True humility helps eliminate worry, because we learn to place our faith, hope, and trust in "His Majesty," as St. Teresa of Avila loved to call God. We trust in *his* ability, and not our own.

In her book *Interior Castle,* speaking of the many things we worry about, St. Teresa writes,

> How many souls the devil must have ruined in this way! They think that all these misgivings, and many more that I could describe, arise from humility, whereas they really come from our lack of self-knowledge. We get a distorted idea of our own nature, and, if we never stop thinking about ourselves, I am not surprised if we experience these fears and others which are still worse. It is for this reason ... that I say we must set our eyes upon Christ our Good, from Whom we shall learn true humility, and also upon His saints.[10]

If we think *too much* of ourselves, we can become prideful and *self*-reliant. If we think *too little* of ourselves, we can *shrink back* from doing what God has called us to do. Even when we are walking with the Lord, trying to maintain a humble and godly life, we can, in moments of temptation and weakness, fall into self-reliance or timidity. Neither ends well.

We need to avoid both self-reliance and self-doubt. We all need to do an examination of conscience each evening to see where we have cooperated with God's grace and where we have let our humanity get in the way of it. And we need to go to confession regularly.

But God does not want us to *dwell* on either our virtues or our sins. If we have successes, we offer them to the Lord for his glory—and move forward. If we have fallen, we apologize, go to confession, receive absolution, do our penance—and move forward! God remembers our sins *no more*!

> As far as the east is from the west, so far does he remove our transgressions from us. (Psalm 103:12)

> For I will be merciful toward their iniquities, and I will remember their sins no more. (Hebrews 8:12)

Listen to these words of Fr. Jacques Philippe. He says that, after we have fallen into temptation and gotten discouraged at our lack of spiritual progress,

> we must make an act of faith and hope, such as: "Thank you, my God, for *all* my past. I firmly believe that you can draw good out of everything I have lived through. I want to have no regrets, and I resolve today to begin from zero, with exactly the same trust as if all my past history were made up of nothing but faithfulness and holiness."[11]

If we were to do this, just think of the bold, loving things we could do for God!

To see how it works when we keep our eyes on Christ, let's take a look at St. Peter.

In the Gospel of Matthew, we read that St. Peter wanted to meet our Lord out on the open water (Matthew 14:25-33). (That alone is a win in my book!) He was a lifelong fisherman, a hardy, robust soul, so he took a leap of faith and got out of the boat. And as long as he kept his eyes on Jesus, he was fine. But as soon as he looked at the waves that surrounded him, he began to sink. Why? Because he knew that in his own strength he could not do what he tried to do. When he took his eyes off of Christ, he panicked.

We too are called to do some "supernatural" living—meaning "above the natural" living. If God says to us, "Come," and he calls us "out of our boat," asking us to trust him even in precarious circumstances, then we must not take our eyes off of Christ, who is the source of our hope, our strength, and our peace. Jesus wants us to *look to him* and place our trust in him and what *he can do*, not what we can do in our own strength, without him.

And when we do decide to take a step of faith and trust God like St. Peter, the Enemy of our souls may come and try to discourage us. If he lies and tells us, "You are not enough, you are going to sink," there is really only one answer for this. Believe it or not, the answer is to agree with him! We are to say, "You are right! In my *own limited strength*, I fail, but in God's *unlimited strength*, I am victorious!" This gets our eyes off ourselves and our own limited capabilities and onto Christ and his endless resources of strength, mercy, and love.

GROW STRONG IN GOD'S WORD

So if the "overwhelmer" comes at you with discouraging jabs, claim what you *can* do by the grace and power of God instead of dwelling on what you can't do. Through Jesus' strength, you can do what God has called you to do! Through the Holy Spirit, you can be strong, brave, powerful, and self-controlled. And because God is with you always, you never need to be afraid.

- "I can do all things in him who strengthens me!" (Philippians 4:13).

- "Be strong and of good courage; be not frightened, neither be dismayed; for the LORD your God is with you wherever you go" (Joshua 1:9).

- "For God did not give us a spirit of timidity but a spirit of power and love and self-control" (2 Timothy 1:7).

- "With the LORD on my side I do not fear. What can man do to me?" (Psalm 118:6).

PRAYER

Dear God, thank you for creating and loving me just as I am. No one knows me better than you or loves me more than you, and for that I am truly grateful. Come, Lord, and fill me anew with yourself. Enlighten my mind with renewed understanding as to who I am, and show me by your grace and Holy Spirit what we can do together. Never let me get discouraged, but help me to place my trust more fully in you and the good things you have in store for those who love you and hope in you. On my own I am weak, but with you I am invincible. Zero plus infinity still equals infinity. Thank you, loving Father! Help me to trust more fully in these truths today. Amen!

CHAPTER FOUR

BE SET FREE:
CAST YOUR CARES ON THE LORD

Cast all your anxieties on him, for he cares about you.

–1 Peter 5:7

So what is the next step in learning to go from worry to wonder?

We use our cares as stepping stones to God. We let each one draw us closer to him.

If you have read the Gospels, you may have heard Jesus' words about the flowers, how beautiful they are and how God provides all they need. And some of us have probably thought, "Well, that's fine if you're a flower." But listen to Jesus' words again:

> And which of you by being anxious can add a cubit to his span of life? If then you are not able to do as small a thing as that, why are you anxious about the rest? Consider the lilies, how they grow; they neither toil nor spin; yet I tell you, even Solomon in all his glory was not clothed like one of these. But if God so clothes the grass which is alive in the field today and tomorrow is thrown into the oven, how

much more will he clothe you, O men of little faith! And do not seek what you are to eat and what you are to drink, *nor be of anxious mind.* For all the nations of the world seek these things; and your Father knows that you need them. Instead, seek his kingdom, and these things shall be yours as well. (Luke 12:25-31, emphasis added)

Jesus tells us, "Do not worry anymore!" Our loving, heavenly Father knows our needs. Even the smallest things are out of our control anyway. So instead of worrying, he asks us to seek the kingdom of God.

We can do that by turning our cares into prayers, voicing our concerns and seeking God and his kingdom *through* them. Amazingly, this allows even our worries and cares to be a vehicle for seeking God and bringing us to our knees in prayer.

St. Peter says, "Cast all your anxieties on him, for he cares about you" (1 Peter 5:7).

How does this work? Specifically and simply, we must *name* our worries. This is very important, because the Enemy of our souls likes to deal in vagueness—which means that if he can make us feel "generally" worried or bothered, he will! Why? Because he hates those who are made in the image and likeness of God. He does everything he can to distract us so that we take our eyes off Christ and keep them on ourselves, on our feelings and our circumstances.

If, instead, we can get at what is *really* bothering us, put our finger on it, and name it specifically, we can get free of the vague notion of feeling "upset." This opens up opportunities for God and us to deal with the concern *together.* Now we can hand it over to God because we know what it is, and we know he cares for us.

GOD IS THE CAPABLE ONE

Here's one fundamental fact that is easy to believe but sometimes remarkably difficult to put into practice: God is a much, much better manager of you and your circumstances than you are. And while you are not to shrink back from your responsibilities, neither are you to worry about things you have no control over.

"So do I have control over anything?" you might ask. "Is there anything I *can* do?"

Yes and no. The word of God states, "If possible, so far as it depends upon you, live peaceably with all" (Romans 12:18). We have a responsibility to do what we can to live at peace with God, with others, and with ourselves. That might mean that we stop putting off something that needs to be done or we start going the extra mile, loving our enemies, doing good to those who hate us, forgiving someone who has wronged us, or asking for forgiveness if we have wronged someone else. It may also include making restitution when possible.

And then, when we have done what we can, we need to let it go. We have to remember that we are not responsible for other people's actions or their response to us. We can only do what we can do, and then we can leave the rest in God's loving and capable hands.

We do our part, and he does his.

Cast Your Worries onto the Lord

1. SETTLE YOURSELF and ask the Lord to show you what *specifically* is bothering you.

2. NAME your worry out loud.

3. ASK YOURSELF these questions:

   • Is this care or worry realistic? Is it true?

   • Have I done my part to solve the problem or help someone else solve it? For example, have

I prepared for a test or interview, made plans for an upcoming event, or gotten the information I need to make a wise decision? In the difficult work of forgiving someone, have I forgiven that person whether or not I feel like it, making an act of the will and placing the person wholly in God's hands?

- If needed, have I gone to confession and been absolved and forgiven? Do I need to apologize to someone or make restitution?

Ask God what your part is to play. And then ask God for the strength to do what, by his grace, only you can do.

If you have done all you can—if there's nothing more you can do—but you still have a nagging feeling of guilt, then it may be that the Enemy of your soul is trying to get your eyes off Jesus and onto yourself. Simply say, "Get behind me, Satan! I am God's beloved child, holy, chosen, redeemed, and capable of victory in him!"

4. For the worries and cares that remain, cup one hand in front of you, and with the other hand, take a worry, name it out loud again, and place it in your cupped hand. Then brush it off completely, casting it onto the Lord. Say, "Here it is, Lord. I give you this care."

Do this for every worry you can think of, naming it and casting it onto him in complete faith and confidence, knowing that God has "got this," and he cares for you.

Remember: You are not sending your worries "off into the universe" in some New Age-y way. You are giving them to your almighty, powerful, loving Father, who cares for you.

When you've given him all your cares, thank him and say, "By your grace, I will not worry anymore. I will keep my eyes on you and off my worries. Please strengthen me and walk with me now."

Know that the Lord receives every one of your worries, because he cares for you.

After doing this, I have found in my own life that God gives the most amazing grace—he allows me to be aware that he is in charge and is accompanying me every step of the way. He does this in one of two ways: He either actually changes my difficult circumstances or he gives me the grace, moment by moment, to get through them as I cling to him in faith.

GROW STRONG IN GOD'S WORD

God expects us to cast our cares on him—they belong in his loving hands. When we hope in him, he renews our strength. When we seek him, he delivers us. And when we cry out, he hears us and saves us:

- "Cast your burden on the LORD, and he will sustain you; he will never permit the righteous to be moved" (Psalm 55:22).

- "They who wait for the LORD shall renew their strength, they shall mount up with wings like eagles, they shall run and not be weary, they shall walk and not faint" (Isaiah 40:31).

- "I sought the LORD, and he answered me, and delivered me from all my fears" (Psalm 34:4).

- "This poor man cried, and the LORD heard him, and saved him out of all his troubles. The angel of the LORD encamps around those who fear him, and delivers them" (Psalm 34:6-7).

PRAYER

Dear Lord, I thank you that your Word is so comforting and encouraging. Please grant me the grace to take King David's prayer as my own:

The LORD is my shepherd,
>   I shall not want;
>   he makes me lie down in green pastures.
He leads me beside still waters;
>   he restores my soul.
He leads me in paths of righteousness
>   for his name's sake.

Even though I walk through the valley of the shadow of death,
>   I fear no evil;
for you are with me;
>   your rod and your staff,
>   they comfort me.

You prepare a table before me
>   in the presence of my enemies;
you anoint my head with oil,
>   my cup overflows.
Surely goodness and mercy shall follow me
>   all the days of my life;
and I shall dwell in the house of the LORD
>   for ever.

–Psalm 23

Thank you, dear Lord. Walk with me and be my Good Shepherd now, I pray.

CHAPTER FIVE

LOOK UP! REJOICE AND BE GRATEFUL

Rejoice in the Lord always; again I will say, Rejoice!

–Philippians 4:4

Don't worry! Pray ... all day (and night).

After casting my cares on the Lord, abandoning myself to him, I will feel much better, at least for a bit. You probably will feel this way, too. If you are like me, you may then start to worry that the feeling won't last.

But God has given us the secret to maintaining the peace that passes all understanding! It is found in Philippians 4.

Let's see what it says:

> Rejoice in the Lord always. I shall say it again: rejoice! Your kindness should be known to all. The Lord is near. Have no anxiety at all, but in everything, by prayer and petition, with thanksgiving, make your requests known to God. Then the peace of God that surpasses all understanding will guard your hearts and minds in Christ Jesus. (Philippians 4:4-7, NAB)

If the worries and cares come back, as they sometimes do, God tells us just what to do in that moment—rejoice! Yes! I know this is counterintuitive, but it is what he says to do. Why? Because once again, it gets our eyes off ourselves, our circumstances, and our worries and onto him, the almighty God who literally loves us to infinity and beyond.

When we fix our eyes on our worries, they get magnified instead of God. And when that happens, whether we realize it or not, we are saying, "My problems are bigger and more powerful than my God." And this makes them loom even larger.

But when we magnify the Lord by praising him and rejoicing, our problems shrink in comparison to the all-powerful God we worship. The game changer is learning to do what the Word of God says to do: rejoice, pray, and be thankful! It not only changes us, orienting us toward God and the ways of God, but also it often changes those around us and even our circumstances.

PRAY AND SING!

There is a story in Scripture where we can see this played out beautifully, in the exciting journey of St. Paul and St. Silas. In Acts 16, we read that when Paul and Silas were in Philippi, a slave woman followed them around for many days. She was possessed by a fortune-telling spirit and kept shouting, "These men are servants of the Most High God, who proclaim to you the way of salvation" (Acts 16:17). Paul became so annoyed at her constant hounding that he cast the spirit out of her. Then the real trouble began. Her "owners," who were used to making money from her ability to tell the future, were furious and had Paul and Silas arrested.

We pick up the story in Acts 16:

> And when they had inflicted many blows upon them, they threw them into prison, charging the jailer to keep them safely. Having received this charge, he put them into the inner prison and fastened their feet in the stocks.

But about midnight Paul and Silas were praying and singing hymns to God, and the prisoners were listening to them, and suddenly there was a great earthquake, so that the foundations of the prison were shaken; and immediately all the doors were opened and every one's chains were unfastened. When the jailer woke and saw that the prison doors were open, he drew his sword and was about to kill himself, supposing that the prisoners had escaped. But Paul cried with a loud voice, "Do not harm yourself, for we are all here." And he called for lights and rushed in, and trembling with fear he fell down before Paul and Silas, and brought them out and said, "Men, what must I do to be saved?" And they said, "Believe in the Lord Jesus, and you will be saved, you and your household." (Acts 16:23-31)

We can see that their circumstances were in fact horrifying. Theirs was not an imaginary concern—they were facing a real and present danger. St. Paul and St. Silas had been beaten and were chained in prison. But what did they choose to do instead of fret, worry, and complain? They chose to *pray and sing*! And what happened? They were freed from the prison, they saved the jailer from suicide, and the jailer and his family became Christians. Who could have planned that except God himself?

We can do the same—we can choose to pray and sing. No matter how terrible our circumstances appear to be or actually are, we can turn our hearts upward and rejoice.

How? When St. Paul tells the Philippians to *rejoice* (and he was the one who was in the prison in Philippi), did the word mean then what it means now?

The Greek word for "rejoice" means "to delight in God's *grace*" or "to experience" or "be conscious" of the grace we have been given.[12] It means to be grateful and express that gratitude joyfully to God. We see St. Paul and St. Silas doing this through prayer and song. We call that *praise*.

This is what the *Catechism* has to say about praise:

Praise is the form of prayer which recognizes most immediately that God is God. It lauds God for his own sake and gives him glory, quite beyond what he does, but simply because HE IS. It shares in the blessed happiness of the pure of heart who love God in faith before seeing him in glory. By praise, the Spirit is joined to our spirits to bear witness that we are children of God, testifying to the only Son in whom we are adopted and by whom we glorify the Father. Praise embraces the other forms of prayer and carries them toward him who is its source and goal: the "one God, the Father, from whom are all things and for whom we exist." (CCC 2639)

I have found that listening to Christian praise music as I am driving, working, cooking, running—just doing life—changes my atmosphere. It directs my thoughts and lifts my spirit to God. When I bless him through my praise, he in turn blesses me back with his Spirit—it is like a spiritual hug. And there are so many ways to praise him! For more inspiration, you can pray the Divine Praises or the *Te Deum*, sing some favorite hymns, or read the Psalms—holy words that bring glory to God.

Jesus said, "And I, when I am lifted up from the earth, will draw all men to myself" (John 12:32). He said this not only about the kind of death he would die but also about what happens daily, moment by moment, when we lift him high with our praise.

We see in the prison story of St. Paul and St. Silas that their praise greatly affected their circumstances. Did their songs move the hand of God to act? I believe so. Their praise certainly affected those around them, including the jailer and his family!

Praise, worship, and prayer are powerful in themselves, and as we practice them, we open ourselves to the changes God wills for us—for ourselves, for others, and for our circumstances. They are powerful tools against the Enemy's schemes.

BE GRATEFUL AND KIND

We see that the word "rejoice" also encompasses the idea of being grateful. St. Paul writes, "Rejoice ... I shall say it again: rejoice!" Why? Because it is so counterintuitive for us. When things are difficult, we tend to think only of our woes and our hurt. Then we withdraw or become defensive and sensitive. We don't think about rejoicing. But we must. And St. Paul goes on to say something even more surprising: "Your kindness should be known to all."

Yipes! When I am upset, "kind" is not how most people would describe me. But Scripture states that when we are in a tight spot, we are not only to rejoice, praising God, but to be kind as well. If rejoicing means to be aware of the grace we have received and grateful for it, kindness means passing that same grace along to others.

St. Paul then says, "The Lord is near. Have no anxiety at all, but in everything, by prayer and petition, with thanksgiving, make your requests known to God."

You may say, "Well, that is much more easily said than done!" But the beauty is this: if we are following St. Paul's instructions, if we are already rejoicing in God's presence, then the Lord is *already* near!

This is amazing—and true. The word "near" in the Greek means not only "nearby" but "ready."[13] What a great promise: God is *ready*! Ready to hear, ready to act, ready to move, ready to calm, ready to love. Ready to do whatever needs to be done in the moment. In a way, that is what grace is—God's readiness to act in the moment to do what needs to be done so that we can take the next step.

Wow! The Lord is near and ready! That is why St. Paul can go on to write, "Have no anxiety at all," which means there is no need to worry.

When we worry, we focus on our immediate concerns. The word for "be anxious" in Greek means "drawn in opposite directions" or "divided into parts."[14] God sees the whole instead of just the parts that trouble us. When we turn our gaze to him, we can trust that he sees all. We can ask that he give us new eyes to see the bigger picture instead of zeroing in on the worrying details. This is incredible. We can move ahead more calmly and confidently now, step-by-step, because we know he is near, seeing and encompassing all, each step, even our future. By focusing on him, we get a much more balanced perspective on life.

St. Paul continues, "In everything, by prayer and petition, with thanksgiving, make your requests known to God."

He says we must *pray and be thankful*! And he says it again to the believers in Thessalonica: "Rejoice always, pray constantly, give thanks in all circumstances; for this is the will of God in Christ Jesus for you" (1 Thessalonians 5:16-18).

So when worries come back at you, acknowledge them, offer them back to the Lord, and keep your gaze on him. Rejoice in him, be kind to others, and pray.

"Then the peace of God that surpasses all understanding will guard your hearts and minds in Christ Jesus," St. Paul tells us.

Wow! What an incredible promise!

GROW STRONG IN GOD'S WORD

When worries return, keep your eyes on the Lord. Take comfort in him. Trust him. Praise him and rejoice in him:

- "Trust in the LORD with all your heart, and do not rely on your own insight. In all your ways acknowledge him, and he will make straight your paths" (Proverbs 3:5-6).

- "I will extol you, my God and King, and bless your name for ever and ever. Every day I will bless you, and praise your name for ever and ever. Great is the LORD, and greatly to be praised, and his greatness is unsearchable" (Psalm 145:1-3).

- "When the cares of my heart are many, your consolations cheer my soul" (Psalm 94:19).

- "Rejoice in your hope, be patient in tribulation, be constant in prayer" (Romans 12:12).

- "This is the day which the LORD has made; let us rejoice and be glad in it" (Psalm 118:24).

PRAYER

This prayer is called the Divine Praises, traditionally prayed after Benediction of the Blessed Sacrament. It is a powerful prayer of blessing and thanksgiving:

Blessed be God.
Blessed be his holy name.
Blessed be Jesus Christ, true God and true man.
Blessed be the name of Jesus.
Blessed be his Most Sacred Heart.
Blessed be his Most Precious Blood.
Blessed be Jesus in the Most Holy Sacrament of the Altar.
Blessed be the Holy Spirit, the Paraclete.
Blessed be the great Mother of God, Mary most holy.
Blessed be her holy and immaculate conception.
Blessed be her glorious assumption.
Blessed be the name of Mary, virgin and mother.
Blessed be St. Joseph, her most chaste spouse.
Blessed be God in his angels and in his saints. Amen.

CHAPTER SIX

STAY IN THE LIGHT: GUIDE YOUR THOUGHTS TO WHAT IS GOOD

Whatever is true ... whatever is pure, whatever is lovely, whatever is gracious, if there is any excellence, if there is anything worthy of praise, think about these things.

–Philippians 4:8

In earlier chapters we have seen how to offer ourselves to the Lord and accept his greatness and our smallness. We have seen how to question each worry, name it, give it to him, and rejoice. We have emphasized how important it is to keep our eyes on him. Now let's look at a way to keep our minds and hearts out of harm's way over the long term.

God tells us in Scripture exactly where we are to let our minds *dwell* if we want to experience lasting peace. As we understand this, our lives will change.

There is so much garbage in this world that fights for real estate in our minds. The garbage can be real—there are many unpleasant realities in this world. But just as we would reject garbage if it were served to us on a plate, we are to reject thoughts that are not healthy for us to dwell on. Instead, we are to take in and embrace thoughts that enable us to flourish.

I used to think that I was at the mercy of whatever thought popped into my head, no matter what that thought was—good, bad, or neutral. If someone made a negative comment to me or even looked at me funny, a self-condemning thought would pop into my head. I would turn it over and over again in my mind. The longer I thought about it, the bigger it would grow. I would begin to get depressed and down on myself because I would judge myself by what I assumed the other person was thinking (even if I had misinterpreted the comment or look).

Whenever I read disheartening or unfortunate news, the same gloomy and unsettled feelings would follow. I would think about the unsettling things again and again, letting them have more and more power in my mind.

HEALTHY THOUGHT BOUNDARIES

Great news! The amazing thing is that we don't have to be controlled by our thoughts. In fact, God asks us to do the opposite. *We* are to take control of our thoughts. We must set healthy boundaries for our thoughts if we want to be free and at peace.

When I first learned about healthy boundaries for my mind, I was taken aback. It did not seem right to censor my thoughts. But after learning that the Enemy of our souls works through what we allow to enter into our thought life, I decided to trust God and try it. St. Paul writes,

> For though we live in the world we are not carrying on a worldly war, for the weapons of our warfare are not worldly but have divine power to destroy strongholds. We destroy arguments and every proud obstacle to the knowledge of God, and take every thought captive to obey Christ. (2 Corinthians 10:3-5)

I had no idea that I could take my thoughts "captive" and make them "obey Christ." By God's grace, believe it or not, this is actually possible.

So what does it mean to "take every thought captive to obey Christ"?

We are to place a kind of filter on our minds, straining out the harmful thoughts and turning our attention to what God says are healthy thoughts. This means learning to recognize and destroy the "arguments" and "proud obstacles" that rise up in our minds against "the knowledge of God." Those obstacles are *anything* that is not ultimately life-giving, for our good, rooted in love, and oriented toward God.

In practice, setting the boundaries is quite simple. We pray to stay alert to our thought life, and when we feel the Holy Spirit giving us a nudge about a particular thought, we ask, "Is this thought true? Is it life-giving? Is it loving?" (And remember that loving may not mean it's easy or feels good. It may mean something tougher, something that requires detachment and discipline.) If a thought is from God, it is always for our good and his glory. And if it is not, we reject it.

We don't reject a lie by struggling and trying not to think about it. Instead, we *replace* it with something better.

What do we replace the lie with? Truth! But not just any truth. Through St. Paul, God tells us the kind of truth where we should allow our thoughts to dwell: freeing, hope-filled truth!

> Finally, brethren, whatever is true, whatever is honorable, whatever is just, whatever is pure, whatever is lovely, whatever is gracious, if there is any excellence, if there is anything worthy of praise, think about these things. What you have learned and received and heard and seen in me, do; and the God of peace will be with you. (Philippians 4:8-9)

We are to dwell in the positive, the beautiful, and the praiseworthy, because truth, beauty, and goodness reflect the very essence of God himself (see CCC 33). This is what Holy Scripture says is life-giving to us.

In practice, you may need to look more closely at what you allow into your mind in the first place. Learn to choose wisely what you download, what you read and look at on the internet, the voices you listen to on social media, the movies you watch, the books you read, and even the people you choose to spend time with. Ask yourself, "Is this a life-giving choice? Will it draw me toward the good? Is it healthy for my heart, my mind, and my soul?"

THE OIL OF GLADNESS

Once you begin to dwell in a "pollution-free" zone, with a pure heart, mind, and soul, it is like breathing fresh, pure oxygen.

The Scriptures say of Christ,

> You loved justice and hated wickedness;
>   therefore God, your God, anointed you
>   with the oil of gladness above your companions.
>   (Hebrews 1:9, NAB)

When we love and dwell in what is right and good, we too are blessed with gladness.

So if you want to experience the "peace of God" and be anointed with the "oil of gladness," let your mind dwell on the good. As the well-known quote attributed to St. Padre Pio says, "Pray, hope, and don't worry." Hope is tied to the goodness, or righteousness, of God. As goodness shapes our thoughts, we find ourselves being more hopeful and walking more closely with him, more and more able to experience real gladness—his joy, his rest, and his peace become ours.

Jesus said, "Peace I leave with you; my peace I give to you; not as the world gives do I give to you. Let not your hearts be troubled, neither let them be afraid" (John 14:27).

His peace is worth the challenge of changing what we let into our minds and hearts. And remember, we are not doing it alone. He is near, and he gives us all we need to do what he asks. He gives us his grace.

That is a powerful promise, something worth changing our thought life for.

GROW STRONG IN GOD'S WORD

The need to turn our thoughts to what is good appears again and again in Scripture. Take encouragement from these verses as you learn to set healthy boundaries for your thoughts:

- "Therefore gird up your minds, be sober, set your hope fully upon the grace that is coming to you at the revelation of Jesus Christ" (1 Peter 1:13).

- "The good man out of the good treasure of his heart produces good, and the evil man out of his evil treasure produces evil; for out of the abundance of the heart his mouth speaks" (Luke 6:45).

- "Set your minds on things that are above, not on things that are on earth" (Colossians 3:2).

- "Let the words of my mouth and the meditation of my heart be acceptable in your sight, O Lord, my rock and my redeemer" (Psalm 19:14).

In the next chapter we will see that God does not leave us defenseless as we deal with our earthly problems. He has given us a supernatural coat of armor to keep us safe.

PRAYER

Dear Lord, you are so wonderfully life-giving! By your grace, your holy Word not only gives me a road map to show me the choicest things on which to dwell—those things that are pure, lovely, gracious, excellent, and worthy of praise. But when I dwell on them, you allow me to experience them through your Holy Spirit within me. Lord, please grant me the desire and the ability to take my thoughts captive, so that my thought life always pleases and honors you. I ask you too for the peace that surpasses all understanding, which you promise as I dwell in unity with you. Thank you, Lord, for hearing my prayer and answering me

CHAPTER SEVEN

ACT IN GOD'S STRENGTH: COURAGEOUSLY STAND FIRM

Be strong in the Lord and in the strength of his might.
Put on the whole armor of God.

–Ephesians 6:10-11

We have spoken of the Enemy of our souls and the lies we must learn to reject in accordance with Sacred Scripture and Sacred Tradition. But who exactly is the Enemy of our souls that we have been talking about?

The idea of evil may seem strange or even bizarre to us. Many people are unaware of the fact that good forces are at work in this world through God's power and that evil forces also exist, which aim to destroy our joy, our peace, and our overall well-being. We do not want to be overly focused on evil, but we also cannot ignore it.

This is how the *Catechism* describes the Enemy of our souls:

> Behind the disobedient choice of our first parents lurks a seductive voice, opposed to God, which makes them fall into death out of envy. Scripture and the Church's Tradition see in this being a fallen angel, called "Satan" or the "devil." The Church teaches that Satan was at first a good angel, made by God: "The devil and the other demons were indeed created naturally good by God, but they became evil by their own doing." (CCC 391)

> The devil (*dia-bolos*) is the one who "throws himself across" God's plan and his work of salvation accomplished in Christ. (CCC 2851)

> [Man] still desires the good, but his nature bears the wound of original sin. He is now inclined to evil and subject to error: "Man is divided in himself. As a result, the whole life of men, both individual and social, shows itself to be a struggle, and a dramatic one, between good and evil, between light and darkness." (CCC 1707)

As God's creation, we yearn for the light, for the good, but because of our fallen nature we all too easily drift away from it. Sometimes we choose what is evil. This struggle, as the *Catechism* says, marks our whole life.

It may seem odd to speak of evil in a book about worry, but we need to understand the connection. First, though, it is important to emphasize that Christ triumphed over evil when he died on the Cross: God "disarmed the principalities and powers and made a public example of them, triumphing over them in him" (Colossians 2:15). Christ has won our victory for us—this is the Good News of the gospel. Through him we have become God's children, loved and protected. And through him we are able to resist evil.

But we must always be on our guard against the powers of darkness, to shield ourselves against the devil's lies and schemes. Worries come from many sources—difficult circumstances, faulty ways of thinking, family habits, chemical imbalances, and emotional vulnerabilities. But they feed on lies. When we worry, we are in effect letting ourselves believe the lies, contradicting what we know is true through Scripture and Church teaching.

Overcoming our worries day by day may seem like fighting small battles, but each battle is important, because it allows us to stand on God's promises and trust him in practice. It helps us pay attention, giving us a chance to discover God's truth and stake our claim in it. And it sets us free to live fully, for the glory of God, the abundant life that Jesus came to give us.

St. Paul describes the battle going on for our hearts and minds every day, writing with confidence in what Christ has gained for us so that we may boldly hold our ground:

> Be strong in the Lord and in the strength of his might. Put on the whole armor of God, that you may be able to stand against the wiles of the devil. For we are not contending against flesh and blood, but against the principalities, against the powers, against the world rulers of this present darkness, against the spiritual hosts of wickedness in the heavenly places. (Ephesians 6:10-12)

I used to think that the good and the evil in the world were more or less equal in strength and power. I imagined that they were off somewhere—I did not know where exactly—just "duking it out." But as Christians we know that the battle is not happening "out there." We are fighting it in the large and small struggles of our lives. And we know that God is *infinitely more powerful* than any evil force. God is the Creator. The Devil and his demons are mere creatures, angels who rebelled against him. There is no contest.

THE ARMOR OF GOD

God has given us the power and the means to stand firm against evil. One way we do this is by putting on God's armor. St. Paul tells us how:

> Take the whole armor of God, that you may be able to withstand in the evil day, and having done all, to stand. Stand therefore, having fastened the belt of truth around your waist, and having put on the

breastplate of righteousness, and having shod your feet with the equipment of the gospel of peace; besides all these, taking the shield of faith, with which you can quench all the flaming darts of the Evil One. And take the helmet of salvation, and the sword of the Spirit, which is the word of God. (Ephesians 6:13-17)

What does it mean to put on the armor of God?

- *"The belt of truth"* comes first. We need to make the truth found in Holy Scripture and the teachings of the Church the basic foundation on which we build our life. Jesus is the Truth, and we must embrace him, and let him embrace us, if we want to stand firm.

- *"The breastplate of righteousness"* is the goodness of Christ that shields our heart. It is his righteousness that protects us. He died on the Cross and made a way for us to be forgiven and set free from the power of sin and death. He gives us the grace, moment by moment, to walk in obedience to all he asks of us.[15]

- *Feet shod with "the gospel of peace"* enable us to walk joyfully with him. This daily walking with God brings us peace, and that peace flows to all who share our lives. Who does not want to run, walk, and stand cushioned by the presence of peace?

- *"The shield of faith"* is our faith in Jesus and his teachings, handed down through his Word and the teachings of his Church. When we carry the shield before us, the Enemy's "flaming darts"—lying whispers, cutting negative remarks, and schemes to undermine us—cannot hurt us. Jesus protects us and keeps us safe. Jesus takes the arrows for us when we place our trust in him.

- *"The helmet of salvation"* is knowing our Savior. The battle of our minds is already won, and Christ is the victor. The helmet of salvation means we know who our Savior is and who we are in him. It means we know what we can do in his strength, for his salvation is complete. When we know and act on this, our minds are protected with an indestructible helmet.

- *"The sword of the Spirit, which is the word of God,"* is Sacred Scripture and the Sacred Tradition of the Church. It is our offensive weapon. With this sword, we can refute the Enemy's lies so that we are not fooled or overcome.

THE POWER OF JESUS' NAME

Scripture tells us about another weapon, too. The name of Jesus, when used reverently and not "taken in vain" (see Exodus 20:7), is the most powerful weapon of all: "For 'every one who calls upon the name of the Lord will be saved'" (Romans 10:13). Because Jesus is the "Word made flesh" (see John 1:14), his name is the most powerful word we can say (see Acts 4:1-20). It was Jesus who defeated our Enemy, the Devil, on the Cross, and in his name we are saved, set free, and healed. The *Catechism* says,

> The name "Jesus" contains all: God and man and the whole economy of creation and salvation. To pray "Jesus" is to invoke him and to call him within us. His name is the only one that contains the presence it signifies. Jesus is the Risen One, and whoever invokes the name of Jesus is welcoming the Son of God who loved him and who gave himself up for him. (CCC 2666)

Our Lord never resists an act of faith when we cry out to him in his name.

Finally, we are to pray at every opportunity and be watchful. As the *Catechism* says, "Against our dullness and laziness, the battle of prayer is that of humble, trusting, and persevering *love*" (CCC 2742).

St. Paul wraps up his teaching on the armor of God by saying, "Pray at all times in the Spirit, with all prayer and supplication" (Ephesians 6:18).

It is through our prayer that we put on God's armor and through our prayer that we defeat the Enemy. So we are to pray "in the Spirit," using whatever gifts of the Spirit God has given us. And in the moments when we can't find the right words, we pray Jesus' powerful name.

GROW STRONG IN GOD'S WORD

Scripture tells us to put on the armor of God, turning away from darkness and arming ourselves with his Word. God himself marches with us, promising us victory and abundant life if we remain faithful.

- "Let us then cast off the works of darkness and put on the armor of light" (Romans 13:12).

- "For the word of God is living and active, sharper than any two-edged sword, piercing to the division of soul and spirit, of joints and marrow, and discerning the thoughts and intentions of the heart" (Hebrews 4:12).

- "Be strong and of good courage, do not fear or be in dread of them: for it is the LORD your God who goes with you; he will not fail you or forsake you" (Deuteronomy 31:6).

- "The thief comes only to steal and kill and destroy; I came that they may have life, and have it abundantly" (John 10:10).

PRAYER

Dear Lord, your Word states,

> Taste and see that the LORD is good;
> > blessed is the stalwart one who takes refuge in him.
> > (Psalm 34:9, NAB)

*I want to be that person, the stalwart one. I want to be blessed.
I want to be the one who stands firm against the attacks of the
Enemy because I take refuge in you. Please change my name
from "timid and faithless" to something new, beautiful, and
different, because I love you and am so grateful for all you
have done for me and in me. I want to know the truth and be
set free! I want to see myself as you see me and live out that
reality. I want to be known as "Courageous!" "Stouthearted!"
"Overcomer!" "Capable!" and "Victorious!" And I know
that by relying on your grace and your Holy Spirit living in
me—by cooperating and being obedient to your Word, acting
on what I know and not what I feel—I can be those things!
Renew my mind to your truth. Free me of my cares, so that
I am no longer worried or afraid. Come, Lord Jesus! Fill me.
Make me new for my good and your great glory.*

PART II

FORTY DAYS
FROM WORRY-TO-WONDER:
A PRACTICE JOURNAL

How to Use This Journal

Forty Days from Worry to Wonder

A Closing Note

HOW TO USE THIS JOURNAL

On the following pages you will find a forty-day journal, a template for learning to go from worry to wonder. Use it to entrust your cares to the Lord every day to "transform habit into nature."[16]

The number forty is used repeatedly throughout the Bible. Noah and his family were in the Ark for forty days and nights. The children of Israel wandered in the desert for forty years. And Christ himself fasted in the wilderness for forty days and nights. The number forty seems about right for transformation.

So shall we try it for forty days and see what God does?

Will you commit to practicing turning from worry to wonder each day? You will never regret one step you take that brings you closer to full trust in God and thus to true freedom in him—freedom from worry, freedom to take delight in the life you have been given.

MAKE A COMMITMENT

Many of us have heard before that taking some sort of concrete action—writing something down, saying something out loud, or telling a friend—increases the chances that we will respect our decision and commit to seeing it through. I encourage you to write your name in the space below and then say the words of the commitment aloud so you can make them your own:

I, _____ , commit, by God's grace, to daily offer myself to God, renew my mind to truth, cast my cares onto God (because he cares for me), and rejoice, pray, and dwell in gratitude.

Here we go! And remember, I am praying for you!

> *Prayer is the best weapon we have,*
> *a key that opens the heart of God.*

–St. Padre Pio

FORTY DAYS
FROM
WORRY
TO
WONDER

Have no anxiety about anything, but in everything by prayer and supplication with thanksgiving let your requests be made known to God.

–Philippians 4:6

DAY 1   **DATE:** _____

- I offer myself to God:

    Here I am, Lord. Please fill me with your Spirit.

- I renew my mind to the truth of who God is and who I am:

    You are my loving, powerful Father, and I am your beloved child.

- I write down today's cares and worries:

_____

_____

_____

_____

_____

Are my worries realistic, Lord? Have I done my part to solve problems or help others solve them? Please show me.

I take each care, name it, and hand it to you. Here it is, Lord! By your grace, I will not worry about it anymore. I will keep my eyes on you and off my worries! Please strengthen me and walk with me now.

- I rejoice and praise God, and I thank him for my many blessings. These are things I am grateful for today:

_____

_____

_____

_____

I praise you, Lord, because you are worthy of all praise!

- I stay in the light, being hopeful, taking my thoughts captive. I dwell on whatever is true, honorable, just, pure, lovely, gracious, excellent, and praiseworthy. When I am tempted to think anxious thoughts, I think about these things instead:

_____

_____

_____

_____

Guide my thinking today, Lord.

- I am geared up! I have put on the full armor of God. I will, by God's grace, courageously stand firm and turn from worry to wonder today!

    Lord, I trust you and I love you above all things. I know that you will protect me today and give me all that I need. I thank you and I praise you.

All battles are first won or lost in the mind.

–attributed to St. Joan of Arc

Have no anxiety about anything, but in everything by prayer and supplication with thanksgiving let your requests be made known to God.

–Philippians 4:6

DAY 2   DATE: _____

- I offer myself to God:

    Here I am, Lord. Please fill me with your Spirit.

- I renew my mind to the truth of who God is and who I am:

    You are my loving, powerful Father, and I am your beloved child.

- I write down today's cares and worries:

_____

_____

_____

_____

Are my worries realistic, Lord? Have I done my part to solve problems or help others solve them? Please show me.

I take each care, name it, and hand it to you. Here it is, Lord! By your grace, I will not worry about it anymore. I will keep my eyes on you and off my worries! Please strengthen me and walk with me now.

- I rejoice and praise God, and I thank him for my many blessings. These are things I am grateful for today:

_____

_____

_____

_____

I praise you, Lord, because you are worthy of all praise!

- I stay in the light, being hopeful, taking my thoughts captive. I dwell on whatever is true, honorable, just, pure, lovely, gracious, excellent, and praiseworthy. When I am tempted to think anxious thoughts, I think about these things instead:

_____

_____

_____

_____

Guide my thinking today, Lord.

- I am geared up! I have put on the full armor of God. I will, by God's grace, courageously stand firm and turn from worry to wonder today!

  Lord, I trust you and I love you above all things. I know that you will protect me today and give me all that I need. I thank you and I praise you.

All battles are first won or lost in the mind.

–attributed to St. Joan of Arc

Have no anxiety about anything, but in everything by prayer and supplication with thanksgiving let your requests be made known to God.

–Philippians 4:6

DAY 3 **DATE:** _____

- I offer myself to God:

    Here I am, Lord. Please fill me with your Spirit.

- I renew my mind to the truth of who God is and who I am:

    You are my loving, powerful Father, and I am your beloved child.

- I write down today's cares and worries:

_____

_____

_____

_____

_____

Are my worries realistic, Lord? Have I done my part to solve problems or help others solve them? Please show me.

I take each care, name it, and hand it to you. Here it is, Lord! By your grace, I will not worry about it anymore. I will keep my eyes on you and off my worries! Please strengthen me and walk with me now.

- I rejoice and praise God, and I thank him for my many blessings. These are things I am grateful for today:

_____

_____

_____

_____

I praise you, Lord, because you are worthy of all praise!

- I stay in the light, being hopeful, taking my thoughts captive. I dwell on whatever is true, honorable, just, pure, lovely, gracious, excellent, and praiseworthy. When I am tempted to think anxious thoughts, I think about these things instead:

_____

_____

_____

_____

Guide my thinking today, Lord.

- I am geared up! I have put on the full armor of God. I will, by God's grace, courageously stand firm and turn from worry to wonder today!

  Lord, I trust you and I love you above all things. I know that you will protect me today and give me all that I need. I thank you and I praise you.

All battles are first won or lost in the mind.

–attributed to St. Joan of Arc

Have no anxiety about anything, but in everything by prayer and supplication with thanksgiving let your requests be made known to God.

–Philippians 4:6

DAY 4   **DATE:** _____

- I offer myself to God:

    Here I am, Lord. Please fill me with your Spirit.

- I renew my mind to the truth of who God is and who I am:

    You are my loving, powerful Father, and I am your beloved child.

- I write down today's cares and worries:

_____

_____

_____

_____

_____

Are my worries realistic, Lord? Have I done my part to solve problems or help others solve them? Please show me.

I take each care, name it, and hand it to you. Here it is, Lord! By your grace, I will not worry about it anymore. I will keep my eyes on you and off my worries! Please strengthen me and walk with me now.

- I rejoice and praise God, and I thank him for my many blessings. These are things I am grateful for today:

_____

_____

_____

_____

I praise you, Lord, because you are worthy of all praise!

- I stay in the light, being hopeful, taking my thoughts captive. I dwell on whatever is true, honorable, just, pure, lovely, gracious, excellent, and praiseworthy. When I am tempted to think anxious thoughts, I think about these things instead:

_____

_____

_____

_____

Guide my thinking today, Lord.

- I am geared up! I have put on the full armor of God. I will, by God's grace, courageously stand firm and turn from worry to wonder today!

    Lord, I trust you and I love you above all things. I know that you will protect me today and give me all that I need. I thank you and I praise you.

All battles are first won or lost in the mind.

—attributed to St. Joan of Arc

Have no anxiety about anything, but in everything by prayer and supplication with thanksgiving let your requests be made known to God.

–Philippians 4:6

DAY 5   **DATE:** _____

- I offer myself to God:

    Here I am, Lord. Please fill me with your Spirit.

- I renew my mind to the truth of who God is and who I am:

    You are my loving, powerful Father, and I am your beloved child.

- I write down today's cares and worries:

_____

_____

_____

_____

_____

Are my worries realistic, Lord? Have I done my part to solve problems or help others solve them? Please show me.

I take each care, name it, and hand it to you. Here it is, Lord! By your grace, I will not worry about it anymore. I will keep my eyes on you and off my worries! Please strengthen me and walk with me now.

- I rejoice and praise God, and I thank him for my many blessings. These are things I am grateful for today:

_____

_____

_____

_____

I praise you, Lord, because you are worthy of all praise!

- I stay in the light, being hopeful, taking my thoughts captive. I dwell on whatever is true, honorable, just, pure, lovely, gracious, excellent, and praiseworthy. When I am tempted to think anxious thoughts, I think about these things instead:

_____

_____

_____

_____

Guide my thinking today, Lord.

- I am geared up! I have put on the full armor of God. I will, by God's grace, courageously stand firm and turn from worry to wonder today!

    Lord, I trust you and I love you above all things. I know that you will protect me today and give me all that I need. I thank you and I praise you.

All battles are first won or lost in the mind.

–attributed to St. Joan of Arc

Have no anxiety about anything, but in everything by prayer and supplication with thanksgiving let your requests be made known to God.

–Philippians 4:6

DAY 6   **DATE:** _____

- I offer myself to God:

    Here I am, Lord. Please fill me with your Spirit.

- I renew my mind to the truth of who God is and who I am:

    You are my loving, powerful Father, and I am your beloved child.

- I write down today's cares and worries:

_____

_____

_____

_____

_____

Are my worries realistic, Lord? Have I done my part to solve problems or help others solve them? Please show me.

I take each care, name it, and hand it to you. Here it is, Lord! By your grace, I will not worry about it anymore. I will keep my eyes on you and off my worries! Please strengthen me and walk with me now.

- I rejoice and praise God, and I thank him for my many blessings. These are things I am grateful for today:

_____

_____

_____

_____

I praise you, Lord, because you are worthy of all praise!

- I stay in the light, being hopeful, taking my thoughts captive. I dwell on whatever is true, honorable, just, pure, lovely, gracious, excellent, and praiseworthy. When I am tempted to think anxious thoughts, I think about these things instead:

_____

_____

_____

_____

Guide my thinking today, Lord.

- I am geared up! I have put on the full armor of God. I will, by God's grace, courageously stand firm and turn from worry to wonder today!

    *Lord, I trust you and I love you above all things. I know
    that you will protect me today and give me all that I need.
    I thank you and I praise you.*

All battles are first won or lost in the mind.

–attributed to St. Joan of Arc

Have no anxiety about anything, but in everything by prayer and supplication with thanksgiving let your requests be made known to God.

–Philippians 4:6

DAY 7   **DATE:** _____

- I offer myself to God:

  Here I am, Lord. Please fill me with your Spirit.

- I renew my mind to the truth of who God is and who I am:

  You are my loving, powerful Father, and I am your beloved child.

- I write down today's cares and worries:

_____

_____

_____

_____

_____

Are my worries realistic, Lord? Have I done my part to solve problems or help others solve them? Please show me.

I take each care, name it, and hand it to you. Here it is, Lord! By your grace, I will not worry about it anymore. I will keep my eyes on you and off my worries! Please strengthen me and walk with me now.

- I rejoice and praise God, and I thank him for my many blessings. These are things I am grateful for today:

_____

_____

_____

_____

I praise you, Lord, because you are worthy of all praise!

- I stay in the light, being hopeful, taking my thoughts captive. I dwell on whatever is true, honorable, just, pure, lovely, gracious, excellent, and praiseworthy. When I am tempted to think anxious thoughts, I think about these things instead:

_____

_____

_____

_____

Guide my thinking today, Lord.

- I am geared up! I have put on the full armor of God. I will, by God's grace, courageously stand firm and turn from worry to wonder today!

  Lord, I trust you and I love you above all things. I know that you will protect me today and give me all that I need. I thank you and I praise you.

All battles are first won or lost in the mind.

–attributed to St. Joan of Arc

Have no anxiety about anything, but in everything by prayer and supplication with thanksgiving let your requests be made known to God.

–Philippians 4:6

DAY 8   **DATE:** _____

- I offer myself to God:

  Here I am, Lord. Please fill me with your Spirit.

- I renew my mind to the truth of who God is and who I am:

  You are my loving, powerful Father, and I am your beloved child.

- I write down today's cares and worries:

_____

_____

_____

_____

_____

Are my worries realistic, Lord? Have I done my part to solve problems or help others solve them? Please show me.

I take each care, name it, and hand it to you. Here it is, Lord! By your grace, I will not worry about it anymore. I will keep my eyes on you and off my worries! Please strengthen me and walk with me now.

- I rejoice and praise God, and I thank him for my many blessings. These are things I am grateful for today:

I praise you, Lord, because you are worthy of all praise!

- I stay in the light, being hopeful, taking my thoughts captive. I dwell on whatever is true, honorable, just, pure, lovely, gracious, excellent, and praiseworthy. When I am tempted to think anxious thoughts, I think about these things instead:

Guide my thinking today, Lord.

- I am geared up! I have put on the full armor of God. I will, by God's grace, courageously stand firm and turn from worry to wonder today!

    Lord, I trust you and I love you above all things. I know that you will protect me today and give me all that I need. I thank you and I praise you.

All battles are first won or lost in the mind.

–attributed to St. Joan of Arc

Have no anxiety about anything, but in everything by prayer and supplication with thanksgiving let your requests be made known to God.

–Philippians 4:6

DAY 9 **DATE:** _____

- I offer myself to God:

  Here I am, Lord. Please fill me with your Spirit.

- I renew my mind to the truth of who God is and who I am:

  You are my loving, powerful Father, and I am your beloved child.

- I write down today's cares and worries:

_____

_____

_____

_____

_____

Are my worries realistic, Lord? Have I done my part to solve problems or help others solve them? Please show me.

I take each care, name it, and hand it to you. Here it is, Lord! By your grace, I will not worry about it anymore. I will keep my eyes on you and off my worries! Please strengthen me and walk with me now.

- I rejoice and praise God, and I thank him for my many blessings. These are things I am grateful for today:

_____

_____

_____

_____

I praise you, Lord, because you are worthy of all praise!

- I stay in the light, being hopeful, taking my thoughts captive. I dwell on whatever is true, honorable, just, pure, lovely, gracious, excellent, and praiseworthy. When I am tempted to think anxious thoughts, I think about these things instead:

_____

_____

_____

_____

Guide my thinking today, Lord.

- I am geared up! I have put on the full armor of God. I will, by God's grace, courageously stand firm and turn from worry to wonder today!

    Lord, I trust you and I love you above all things. I know that you will protect me today and give me all that I need. I thank you and I praise you.

All battles are first won or lost in the mind.

–attributed to St. Joan of Arc

Have no anxiety about anything, but in everything by prayer and supplication with thanksgiving let your requests be made known to God.

–Philippians 4:6

DAY 10   **DATE:** _____

- I offer myself to God:

  Here I am, Lord. Please fill me with your Spirit.

- I renew my mind to the truth of who God is and who I am:

  You are my loving, powerful Father, and I am your beloved child.

- I write down today's cares and worries:

_____

_____

_____

_____

_____

Are my worries realistic, Lord? Have I done my part to solve problems or help others solve them? Please show me.

I take each care, name it, and hand it to you. Here it is, Lord! By your grace, I will not worry about it anymore. I will keep my eyes on you and off my worries! Please strengthen me and walk with me now.

- I rejoice and praise God, and I thank him for my many blessings. These are things I am grateful for today:

_____

_____

_____

_____

I praise you, Lord, because you are worthy of all praise!

- I stay in the light, being hopeful, taking my thoughts captive. I dwell on whatever is true, honorable, just, pure, lovely, gracious, excellent, and praiseworthy. When I am tempted to think anxious thoughts, I think about these things instead:

_____

_____

_____

_____

Guide my thinking today, Lord.

- I am geared up! I have put on the full armor of God. I will, by God's grace, courageously stand firm and turn from worry to wonder today!

  Lord, I trust you and I love you above all things. I know that you will protect me today and give me all that I need. I thank you and I praise you.

All battles are first won or lost in the mind.

–attributed to St. Joan of Arc

Have no anxiety about anything, but in everything by prayer and supplication with thanksgiving let your requests be made known to God.

–Philippians 4:6

DAY 11   **DATE:** _____

- I offer myself to God:

    Here I am, Lord. Please fill me with your Spirit.

- I renew my mind to the truth of who God is and who I am:

    You are my loving, powerful Father, and I am your beloved child.

- I write down today's cares and worries:

_____

_____

_____

_____

_____

Are my worries realistic, Lord? Have I done my part to solve problems or help others solve them? Please show me.

I take each care, name it, and hand it to you. Here it is, Lord! By your grace, I will not worry about it anymore. I will keep my eyes on you and off my worries! Please strengthen me and walk with me now.

- I rejoice and praise God, and I thank him for my many blessings. These are things I am grateful for today:

I praise you, Lord, because you are worthy of all praise!

- I stay in the light, being hopeful, taking my thoughts captive. I dwell on whatever is true, honorable, just, pure, lovely, gracious, excellent, and praiseworthy. When I am tempted to think anxious thoughts, I think about these things instead:

Guide my thinking today, Lord.

- I am geared up! I have put on the full armor of God. I will, by God's grace, courageously stand firm and turn from worry to wonder today!

   Lord, I trust you and I love you above all things. I know that you will protect me today and give me all that I need. I thank you and I praise you.

   All battles are first won or lost in the mind.

   –attributed to St. Joan of Arc

Have no anxiety about anything, but in everything by prayer and supplication with thanksgiving let your requests be made known to God.

–Philippians 4:6

DAY 12   **DATE:** _____

- I offer myself to God:

    Here I am, Lord. Please fill me with your Spirit.

- I renew my mind to the truth of who God is and who I am:

    You are my loving, powerful Father, and I am your beloved child.

- I write down today's cares and worries:

_____

_____

_____

_____

_____

Are my worries realistic, Lord? Have I done my part to solve problems or help others solve them? Please show me.

I take each care, name it, and hand it to you. Here it is, Lord! By your grace, I will not worry about it anymore. I will keep my eyes on you and off my worries! Please strengthen me and walk with me now.

- I rejoice and praise God, and I thank him for my many blessings. These are things I am grateful for today:

_____

_____

_____

I praise you, Lord, because you are worthy of all praise!

- I stay in the light, being hopeful, taking my thoughts captive. I dwell on whatever is true, honorable, just, pure, lovely, gracious, excellent, and praiseworthy. When I am tempted to think anxious thoughts, I think about these things instead:

_____

_____

_____

Guide my thinking today, Lord.

- I am geared up! I have put on the full armor of God. I will, by God's grace, courageously stand firm and turn from worry to wonder today!

  Lord, I trust you and I love you above all things. I know that you will protect me today and give me all that I need. I thank you and I praise you.

All battles are first won or lost in the mind.

–attributed to St. Joan of Arc

Have no anxiety about anything, but in everything by prayer and supplication with thanksgiving let your requests be made known to God.

–Philippians 4:6

DAY 13   **DATE:** _____

- I offer myself to God:

    Here I am, Lord. Please fill me with your Spirit.

- I renew my mind to the truth of who God is and who I am:

    You are my loving, powerful Father, and I am your beloved child.

- I write down today's cares and worries:

_____

_____

_____

_____

_____

Are my worries realistic, Lord? Have I done my part to solve problems or help others solve them? Please show me.

I take each care, name it, and hand it to you. Here it is, Lord! By your grace, I will not worry about it anymore. I will keep my eyes on you and off my worries! Please strengthen me and walk with me now.

- I rejoice and praise God, and I thank him for my many blessings.
  These are things I am grateful for today:

_____

_____

_____

_____

I praise you, Lord, because you are worthy of all praise!

- I stay in the light, being hopeful, taking my thoughts captive.
  I dwell on whatever is true, honorable, just, pure, lovely, gracious,
  excellent, and praiseworthy. When I am tempted to think anxious
  thoughts, I think about these things instead:

_____

_____

_____

_____

Guide my thinking today, Lord.

- I am geared up! I have put on the full armor of God. I will, by
  God's grace, courageously stand firm and turn from worry to
  wonder today!

  *Lord, I trust you and I love you above all things. I know
  that you will protect me today and give me all that I need.
  I thank you and I praise you.*

All battles are first won or lost in the mind.

–attributed to St. Joan of Arc

Have no anxiety about anything, but in everything by prayer and supplication with thanksgiving let your requests be made known to God.

–Philippians 4:6

DAY 14   **DATE:** _____

- I offer myself to God:

     Here I am, Lord. Please fill me with your Spirit.

- I renew my mind to the truth of who God is and who I am:

     You are my loving, powerful Father, and I am your beloved child.

- I write down today's cares and worries:

_____

_____

_____

_____

_____

Are my worries realistic, Lord? Have I done my part to solve problems or help others solve them? Please show me.

I take each care, name it, and hand it to you. Here it is, Lord! By your grace, I will not worry about it anymore. I will keep my eyes on you and off my worries! Please strengthen me and walk with me now.

- I rejoice and praise God, and I thank him for my many blessings. These are things I am grateful for today:

_____

_____

_____

_____

  I praise you, Lord, because you are worthy of all praise!

- I stay in the light, being hopeful, taking my thoughts captive. I dwell on whatever is true, honorable, just, pure, lovely, gracious, excellent, and praiseworthy. When I am tempted to think anxious thoughts, I think about these things instead:

_____

_____

_____

_____

  Guide my thinking today, Lord.

- I am geared up! I have put on the full armor of God. I will, by God's grace, courageously stand firm and turn from worry to wonder today!

  Lord, I trust you and I love you above all things. I know that you will protect me today and give me all that I need. I thank you and I praise you.

  All battles are first won or lost in the mind.

  –attributed to St. Joan of Arc

Have no anxiety about anything, but in everything by prayer and supplication with thanksgiving let your requests be made known to God.

–Philippians 4:6

DAY 15   **DATE:** _____

- I offer myself to God:

    Here I am, Lord. Please fill me with your Spirit.

- I renew my mind to the truth of who God is and who I am:

    You are my loving, powerful Father, and I am your beloved child.

- I write down today's cares and worries:

_____

_____

_____

_____

_____

Are my worries realistic, Lord? Have I done my part to solve problems or help others solve them? Please show me.

I take each care, name it, and hand it to you. Here it is, Lord! By your grace, I will not worry about it anymore. I will keep my eyes on you and off my worries! Please strengthen me and walk with me now.

- I rejoice and praise God, and I thank him for my many blessings. These are things I am grateful for today:

_____

_____

_____

_____

I praise you, Lord, because you are worthy of all praise!

- I stay in the light, being hopeful, taking my thoughts captive. I dwell on whatever is true, honorable, just, pure, lovely, gracious, excellent, and praiseworthy. When I am tempted to think anxious thoughts, I think about these things instead:

_____

_____

_____

_____

Guide my thinking today, Lord.

- I am geared up! I have put on the full armor of God. I will, by God's grace, courageously stand firm and turn from worry to wonder today!

    Lord, I trust you and I love you above all things. I know that you will protect me today and give me all that I need. I thank you and I praise you.

All battles are first won or lost in the mind.

–attributed to St. Joan of Arc

Have no anxiety about anything, but in everything by prayer and supplication with thanksgiving let your requests be made known to God.

–Philippians 4:6

DAY 16   **DATE:** _____

- I offer myself to God:

    Here I am, Lord. Please fill me with your Spirit.

- I renew my mind to the truth of who God is and who I am:

    You are my loving, powerful Father, and I am your beloved child.

- I write down today's cares and worries:

_____

_____

_____

_____

Are my worries realistic, Lord? Have I done my part to solve problems or help others solve them? Please show me.

I take each care, name it, and hand it to you. Here it is, Lord! By your grace, I will not worry about it anymore. I will keep my eyes on you and off my worries! Please strengthen me and walk with me now.

- I rejoice and praise God, and I thank him for my many blessings. These are things I am grateful for today:

_____

_____

_____

_____

I praise you, Lord, because you are worthy of all praise!

- I stay in the light, being hopeful, taking my thoughts captive. I dwell on whatever is true, honorable, just, pure, lovely, gracious, excellent, and praiseworthy. When I am tempted to think anxious thoughts, I think about these things instead:

_____

_____

_____

_____

Guide my thinking today, Lord.

- I am geared up! I have put on the full armor of God. I will, by God's grace, courageously stand firm and turn from worry to wonder today!

  Lord, I trust you and I love you above all things. I know that you will protect me today and give me all that I need. I thank you and I praise you.

All battles are first won or lost in the mind.

−attributed to St. Joan of Arc

Have no anxiety about anything, but in everything by prayer and supplication with thanksgiving let your requests be made known to God.

–Philippians 4:6

DAY 17   **DATE:** _____

- I offer myself to God:

  Here I am, Lord. Please fill me with your Spirit.

- I renew my mind to the truth of who God is and who I am:

  You are my loving, powerful Father, and I am your beloved child.

- I write down today's cares and worries:

_____

_____

_____

_____

_____

Are my worries realistic, Lord? Have I done my part to solve problems or help others solve them? Please show me.

I take each care, name it, and hand it to you. Here it is, Lord! By your grace, I will not worry about it anymore. I will keep my eyes on you and off my worries! Please strengthen me and walk with me now.

- I rejoice and praise God, and I thank him for my many blessings. These are things I am grateful for today:

_____

_____

_____

_____

I praise you, Lord, because you are worthy of all praise!

- I stay in the light, being hopeful, taking my thoughts captive. I dwell on whatever is true, honorable, just, pure, lovely, gracious, excellent, and praiseworthy. When I am tempted to think anxious thoughts, I think about these things instead:

_____

_____

_____

_____

Guide my thinking today, Lord.

- I am geared up! I have put on the full armor of God. I will, by God's grace, courageously stand firm and turn from worry to wonder today!

    Lord, I trust you and I love you above all things. I know that you will protect me today and give me all that I need. I thank you and I praise you.

All battles are first won or lost in the mind.

–attributed to St. Joan of Arc

Have no anxiety about anything, but in everything by prayer and supplication with thanksgiving let your requests be made known to God.

–Philippians 4:6

DAY 18　　　　　　**DATE:** _____

- I offer myself to God:

  Here I am, Lord. Please fill me with your Spirit.

- I renew my mind to the truth of who God is and who I am:

  You are my loving, powerful Father, and I am your beloved child.

- I write down today's cares and worries:

_____

_____

_____

_____

_____

Are my worries realistic, Lord? Have I done my part to solve problems or help others solve them? Please show me.

I take each care, name it, and hand it to you. Here it is, Lord! By your grace, I will not worry about it anymore. I will keep my eyes on you and off my worries! Please strengthen me and walk with me now.

- I rejoice and praise God, and I thank him for my many blessings. These are things I am grateful for today:

_____

_____

_____

_____

I praise you, Lord, because you are worthy of all praise!

- I stay in the light, being hopeful, taking my thoughts captive. I dwell on whatever is true, honorable, just, pure, lovely, gracious, excellent, and praiseworthy. When I am tempted to think anxious thoughts, I think about these things instead:

_____

_____

_____

_____

Guide my thinking today, Lord.

- I am geared up! I have put on the full armor of God. I will, by God's grace, courageously stand firm and turn from worry to wonder today!

  Lord, I trust you and I love you above all things. I know that you will protect me today and give me all that I need. I thank you and I praise you.

All battles are first won or lost in the mind.

–attributed to St. Joan of Arc

Have no anxiety about anything, but in everything by prayer and supplication with thanksgiving let your requests be made known to God.

–Philippians 4:6

DAY 19   **DATE:** _____

- I offer myself to God:

  Here I am, Lord. Please fill me with your Spirit.

- I renew my mind to the truth of who God is and who I am:

  You are my loving, powerful Father, and I am your beloved child.

- I write down today's cares and worries:

_____

_____

_____

_____

_____

Are my worries realistic, Lord? Have I done my part to solve problems or help others solve them? Please show me.

I take each care, name it, and hand it to you. Here it is, Lord! By your grace, I will not worry about it anymore. I will keep my eyes on you and off my worries! Please strengthen me and walk with me now.

- I rejoice and praise God, and I thank him for my many blessings. These are things I am grateful for today:

_____

_____

_____

_____

I praise you, Lord, because you are worthy of all praise!

- I stay in the light, being hopeful, taking my thoughts captive. I dwell on whatever is true, honorable, just, pure, lovely, gracious, excellent, and praiseworthy. When I am tempted to think anxious thoughts, I think about these things instead:

_____

_____

_____

_____

Guide my thinking today, Lord.

- I am geared up! I have put on the full armor of God. I will, by God's grace, courageously stand firm and turn from worry to wonder today!

  Lord, I trust you and I love you above all things. I know that you will protect me today and give me all that I need. I thank you and I praise you.

All battles are first won or lost in the mind.

–attributed to St. Joan of Arc

Have no anxiety about anything, but in everything by prayer and supplication with thanksgiving let your requests be made known to God.

–Philippians 4:6

DAY 20   **DATE:** _____

- I offer myself to God:

    Here I am, Lord. Please fill me with your Spirit.

- I renew my mind to the truth of who God is and who I am:

    You are my loving, powerful Father, and I am your beloved child.

- I write down today's cares and worries:

_____

_____

_____

_____

Are my worries realistic, Lord? Have I done my part to solve problems or help others solve them? Please show me.

I take each care, name it, and hand it to you. Here it is, Lord! By your grace, I will not worry about it anymore. I will keep my eyes on you and off my worries! Please strengthen me and walk with me now.

- I rejoice and praise God, and I thank him for my many blessings. These are things I am grateful for today:

_____

_____

_____

_____

I praise you, Lord, because you are worthy of all praise!

- I stay in the light, being hopeful, taking my thoughts captive. I dwell on whatever is true, honorable, just, pure, lovely, gracious, excellent, and praiseworthy. When I am tempted to think anxious thoughts, I think about these things instead:

_____

_____

_____

_____

Guide my thinking today, Lord.

- I am geared up! I have put on the full armor of God. I will, by God's grace, courageously stand firm and turn from worry to wonder today!

    Lord, I trust you and I love you above all things. I know that you will protect me today and give me all that I need. I thank you and I praise you.

All battles are first won or lost in the mind.

—attributed to St. Joan of Arc

Have no anxiety about anything, but in everything by prayer and supplication with thanksgiving let your requests be made known to God.

–Philippians 4:6

DAY 21   **DATE:** _____

- I offer myself to God:

    Here I am, Lord. Please fill me with your Spirit.

- I renew my mind to the truth of who God is and who I am:

    You are my loving, powerful Father, and I am your beloved child.

- I write down today's cares and worries:

_____

_____

_____

_____

_____

Are my worries realistic, Lord? Have I done my part to solve problems or help others solve them? Please show me.

I take each care, name it, and hand it to you. Here it is, Lord! By your grace, I will not worry about it anymore. I will keep my eyes on you and off my worries! Please strengthen me and walk with me now.

- I rejoice and praise God, and I thank him for my many blessings. These are things I am grateful for today:

_____

_____

_____

_____

I praise you, Lord, because you are worthy of all praise!

- I stay in the light, being hopeful, taking my thoughts captive. I dwell on whatever is true, honorable, just, pure, lovely, gracious, excellent, and praiseworthy. When I am tempted to think anxious thoughts, I think about these things instead:

_____

_____

_____

_____

Guide my thinking today, Lord.

- I am geared up! I have put on the full armor of God. I will, by God's grace, courageously stand firm and turn from worry to wonder today!

    Lord, I trust you and I love you above all things. I know that you will protect me today and give me all that I need. I thank you and I praise you.

All battles are first won or lost in the mind.

–attributed to St. Joan of Arc

Have no anxiety about anything, but in everything by prayer and supplication with thanksgiving let your requests be made known to God.

–Philippians 4:6

DAY 22   **DATE:** _____

- I offer myself to God:

    Here I am, Lord. Please fill me with your Spirit.

- I renew my mind to the truth of who God is and who I am:

    You are my loving, powerful Father, and I am your beloved child.

- I write down today's cares and worries:

_____

_____

_____

_____

_____

Are my worries realistic, Lord? Have I done my part to solve problems or help others solve them? Please show me.

I take each care, name it, and hand it to you. Here it is, Lord! By your grace, I will not worry about it anymore. I will keep my eyes on you and off my worries! Please strengthen me and walk with me now.

- I rejoice and praise God, and I thank him for my many blessings. These are things I am grateful for today:

I praise you, Lord, because you are worthy of all praise!

- I stay in the light, being hopeful, taking my thoughts captive. I dwell on whatever is true, honorable, just, pure, lovely, gracious, excellent, and praiseworthy. When I am tempted to think anxious thoughts, I think about these things instead:

Guide my thinking today, Lord.

- I am geared up! I have put on the full armor of God. I will, by God's grace, courageously stand firm and turn from worry to wonder today!

    Lord, I trust you and I love you above all things. I know that you will protect me today and give me all that I need. I thank you and I praise you.

All battles are first won or lost in the mind.

–attributed to St. Joan of Arc

Have no anxiety about anything, but in everything by prayer and supplication with thanksgiving let your requests be made known to God.

–Philippians 4:6

DAY 23   **DATE:** _____

- I offer myself to God:

    Here I am, Lord. Please fill me with your Spirit.

- I renew my mind to the truth of who God is and who I am:

    You are my loving, powerful Father, and I am your beloved child.

- I write down today's cares and worries:

_____

_____

_____

_____

_____

Are my worries realistic, Lord? Have I done my part to solve problems or help others solve them? Please show me.

I take each care, name it, and hand it to you. Here it is, Lord! By your grace, I will not worry about it anymore. I will keep my eyes on you and off my worries! Please strengthen me and walk with me now.

- I rejoice and praise God, and I thank him for my many blessings. These are things I am grateful for today:

_____

_____

_____

I praise you, Lord, because you are worthy of all praise!

- I stay in the light, being hopeful, taking my thoughts captive. I dwell on whatever is true, honorable, just, pure, lovely, gracious, excellent, and praiseworthy. When I am tempted to think anxious thoughts, I think about these things instead:

_____

_____

_____

Guide my thinking today, Lord.

- I am geared up! I have put on the full armor of God. I will, by God's grace, courageously stand firm and turn from worry to wonder today!

  Lord, I trust you and I love you above all things. I know that you will protect me today and give me all that I need. I thank you and I praise you.

All battles are first won or lost in the mind.

—attributed to St. Joan of Arc

Have no anxiety about anything, but in everything by prayer and supplication with thanksgiving let your requests be made known to God.

−Philippians 4:6

DAY 24 **DATE:** _____

- I offer myself to God:

    Here I am, Lord. Please fill me with your Spirit.

- I renew my mind to the truth of who God is and who I am:

    You are my loving, powerful Father, and I am your beloved child.

- I write down today's cares and worries:

_____

_____

_____

_____

_____

Are my worries realistic, Lord? Have I done my part to solve problems or help others solve them? Please show me.

I take each care, name it, and hand it to you. Here it is, Lord! By your grace, I will not worry about it anymore. I will keep my eyes on you and off my worries! Please strengthen me and walk with me now.

- I rejoice and praise God, and I thank him for my many blessings. These are things I am grateful for today:

_____

_____

_____

_____

I praise you, Lord, because you are worthy of all praise!

- I stay in the light, being hopeful, taking my thoughts captive. I dwell on whatever is true, honorable, just, pure, lovely, gracious, excellent, and praiseworthy. When I am tempted to think anxious thoughts, I think about these things instead:

_____

_____

_____

_____

Guide my thinking today, Lord.

- I am geared up! I have put on the full armor of God. I will, by God's grace, courageously stand firm and turn from worry to wonder today!

    Lord, I trust you and I love you above all things. I know that you will protect me today and give me all that I need. I thank you and I praise you.

All battles are first won or lost in the mind.

—attributed to St. Joan of Arc

Have no anxiety about anything, but in everything by prayer and supplication with thanksgiving let your requests be made known to God.

–Philippians 4:6

DAY 25 **DATE:** _____

- I offer myself to God:

    Here I am, Lord. Please fill me with your Spirit.

- I renew my mind to the truth of who God is and who I am:

    You are my loving, powerful Father, and I am your beloved child.

- I write down today's cares and worries:

_____

_____

_____

_____

_____

Are my worries realistic, Lord? Have I done my part to solve problems or help others solve them? Please show me.

I take each care, name it, and hand it to you. Here it is, Lord! By your grace, I will not worry about it anymore. I will keep my eyes on you and off my worries! Please strengthen me and walk with me now.

- I rejoice and praise God, and I thank him for my many blessings. These are things I am grateful for today:

_____

_____

_____

_____

I praise you, Lord, because you are worthy of all praise!

- I stay in the light, being hopeful, taking my thoughts captive. I dwell on whatever is true, honorable, just, pure, lovely, gracious, excellent, and praiseworthy. When I am tempted to think anxious thoughts, I think about these things instead:

_____

_____

_____

_____

Guide my thinking today, Lord.

- I am geared up! I have put on the full armor of God. I will, by God's grace, courageously stand firm and turn from worry to wonder today!

    Lord, I trust you and I love you above all things. I know that you will protect me today and give me all that I need. I thank you and I praise you.

All battles are first won or lost in the mind.

–attributed to St. Joan of Arc

Have no anxiety about anything, but in everything by prayer and supplication with thanksgiving let your requests be made known to God.

–Philippians 4:6

DAY 26   **DATE:** _____

- I offer myself to God:

    Here I am, Lord. Please fill me with your Spirit.

- I renew my mind to the truth of who God is and who I am:

    You are my loving, powerful Father, and I am your beloved child.

- I write down today's cares and worries:

_____

_____

_____

_____

_____

Are my worries realistic, Lord? Have I done my part to solve problems or help others solve them? Please show me.

I take each care, name it, and hand it to you. Here it is, Lord! By your grace, I will not worry about it anymore. I will keep my eyes on you and off my worries! Please strengthen me and walk with me now.

- I rejoice and praise God, and I thank him for my many blessings. These are things I am grateful for today:

_____

_____

_____

_____

I praise you, Lord, because you are worthy of all praise!

- I stay in the light, being hopeful, taking my thoughts captive. I dwell on whatever is true, honorable, just, pure, lovely, gracious, excellent, and praiseworthy. When I am tempted to think anxious thoughts, I think about these things instead:

_____

_____

_____

_____

Guide my thinking today, Lord.

- I am geared up! I have put on the full armor of God. I will, by God's grace, courageously stand firm and turn from worry to wonder today!

  Lord, I trust you and I love you above all things. I know that you will protect me today and give me all that I need. I thank you and I praise you.

All battles are first won or lost in the mind.

–attributed to St. Joan of Arc

Have no anxiety about anything, but in everything by prayer and supplication with thanksgiving let your requests be made known to God.

–Philippians 4:6

DAY 27   **DATE:** _____

- I offer myself to God:

    Here I am, Lord. Please fill me with your Spirit.

- I renew my mind to the truth of who God is and who I am:

    You are my loving, powerful Father, and I am your beloved child.

- I write down today's cares and worries:

_____

_____

_____

_____

_____

Are my worries realistic, Lord? Have I done my part to solve problems or help others solve them? Please show me.

I take each care, name it, and hand it to you. Here it is, Lord! By your grace, I will not worry about it anymore. I will keep my eyes on you and off my worries! Please strengthen me and walk with me now.

- I rejoice and praise God, and I thank him for my many blessings. These are things I am grateful for today:

_____

_____

_____

_____

I praise you, Lord, because you are worthy of all praise!

- I stay in the light, being hopeful, taking my thoughts captive. I dwell on whatever is true, honorable, just, pure, lovely, gracious, excellent, and praiseworthy. When I am tempted to think anxious thoughts, I think about these things instead:

_____

_____

_____

_____

Guide my thinking today, Lord.

- I am geared up! I have put on the full armor of God. I will, by God's grace, courageously stand firm and turn from worry to wonder today!

    Lord, I trust you and I love you above all things. I know that you will protect me today and give me all that I need. I thank you and I praise you.

All battles are first won or lost in the mind.

−attributed to St. Joan of Arc

Have no anxiety about anything, but in everything by prayer and supplication with thanksgiving let your requests be made known to God.

–Philippians 4:6

DAY 28   **DATE:** _____

- I offer myself to God:

  Here I am, Lord. Please fill me with your Spirit.

- I renew my mind to the truth of who God is and who I am:

  You are my loving, powerful Father, and I am your beloved child.

- I write down today's cares and worries:

_____

_____

_____

_____

_____

Are my worries realistic, Lord? Have I done my part to solve problems or help others solve them? Please show me.

I take each care, name it, and hand it to you. Here it is, Lord! By your grace, I will not worry about it anymore. I will keep my eyes on you and off my worries! Please strengthen me and walk with me now.

- I rejoice and praise God, and I thank him for my many blessings. These are things I am grateful for today:

_____

_____

_____

_____

I praise you, Lord, because you are worthy of all praise!

- I stay in the light, being hopeful, taking my thoughts captive. I dwell on whatever is true, honorable, just, pure, lovely, gracious, excellent, and praiseworthy. When I am tempted to think anxious thoughts, I think about these things instead:

_____

_____

_____

_____

Guide my thinking today, Lord.

- I am geared up! I have put on the full armor of God. I will, by God's grace, courageously stand firm and turn from worry to wonder today!

   Lord, I trust you and I love you above all things. I know that you will protect me today and give me all that I need. I thank you and I praise you.

All battles are first won or lost in the mind.

—attributed to St. Joan of Arc

Have no anxiety about anything, but in everything by prayer and supplication with thanksgiving let your requests be made known to God.

–Philippians 4:6

DAY 29   **DATE:** _____

- I offer myself to God:

    Here I am, Lord. Please fill me with your Spirit.

- I renew my mind to the truth of who God is and who I am:

    You are my loving, powerful Father, and I am your beloved child.

- I write down today's cares and worries:

_____

_____

_____

_____

_____

Are my worries realistic, Lord? Have I done my part to solve problems or help others solve them? Please show me.

I take each care, name it, and hand it to you. Here it is, Lord! By your grace, I will not worry about it anymore. I will keep my eyes on you and off my worries! Please strengthen me and walk with me now.

- I rejoice and praise God, and I thank him for my many blessings. These are things I am grateful for today:

_____

_____

_____

_____

I praise you, Lord, because you are worthy of all praise!

- I stay in the light, being hopeful, taking my thoughts captive. I dwell on whatever is true, honorable, just, pure, lovely, gracious, excellent, and praiseworthy. When I am tempted to think anxious thoughts, I think about these things instead:

_____

_____

_____

_____

Guide my thinking today, Lord.

- I am geared up! I have put on the full armor of God. I will, by God's grace, courageously stand firm and turn from worry to wonder today!

   Lord, I trust you and I love you above all things. I know that you will protect me today and give me all that I need. I thank you and I praise you.

All battles are first won or lost in the mind.

–attributed to St. Joan of Arc

Have no anxiety about anything, but in everything by prayer and supplication with thanksgiving let your requests be made known to God.

–Philippians 4:6

DAY 30 **DATE:** _____

- I offer myself to God:

    Here I am, Lord. Please fill me with your Spirit.

- I renew my mind to the truth of who God is and who I am:

    You are my loving, powerful Father, and I am your beloved child.

- I write down today's cares and worries:

_____

_____

_____

_____

_____

Are my worries realistic, Lord? Have I done my part to solve problems or help others solve them? Please show me.

I take each care, name it, and hand it to you. Here it is, Lord! By your grace, I will not worry about it anymore. I will keep my eyes on you and off my worries! Please strengthen me and walk with me now.

- I rejoice and praise God, and I thank him for my many blessings. These are things I am grateful for today:

_____

_____

_____

_____

I praise you, Lord, because you are worthy of all praise!

- I stay in the light, being hopeful, taking my thoughts captive. I dwell on whatever is true, honorable, just, pure, lovely, gracious, excellent, and praiseworthy. When I am tempted to think anxious thoughts, I think about these things instead:

_____

_____

_____

_____

Guide my thinking today, Lord.

- I am geared up! I have put on the full armor of God. I will, by God's grace, courageously stand firm and turn from worry to wonder today!

  Lord, I trust you and I love you above all things. I know that you will protect me today and give me all that I need. I thank you and I praise you.

All battles are first won or lost in the mind.

–attributed to St. Joan of Arc

Have no anxiety about anything, but in everything by prayer and supplication with thanksgiving let your requests be made known to God.

–Philippians 4:6

DAY 31   **DATE:** _____

- I offer myself to God:

    Here I am, Lord. Please fill me with your Spirit.

- I renew my mind to the truth of who God is and who I am:

    You are my loving, powerful Father, and I am your beloved child.

- I write down today's cares and worries:

_____

_____

_____

_____

_____

Are my worries realistic, Lord? Have I done my part to solve problems or help others solve them? Please show me.

I take each care, name it, and hand it to you. Here it is, Lord! By your grace, I will not worry about it anymore. I will keep my eyes on you and off my worries! Please strengthen me and walk with me now.

- I rejoice and praise God, and I thank him for my many blessings. These are things I am grateful for today:

_____

_____

_____

_____

I praise you, Lord, because you are worthy of all praise!

- I stay in the light, being hopeful, taking my thoughts captive. I dwell on whatever is true, honorable, just, pure, lovely, gracious, excellent, and praiseworthy. When I am tempted to think anxious thoughts, I think about these things instead:

_____

_____

_____

_____

Guide my thinking today, Lord.

- I am geared up! I have put on the full armor of God. I will, by God's grace, courageously stand firm and turn from worry to wonder today!

    Lord, I trust you and I love you above all things. I know that you will protect me today and give me all that I need. I thank you and I praise you.

All battles are first won or lost in the mind.

–attributed to St. Joan of Arc

Have no anxiety about anything, but in everything by prayer and supplication with thanksgiving let your requests be made known to God.

–Philippians 4:6

DAY 32   **DATE:** _____

- I offer myself to God:

    Here I am, Lord. Please fill me with your Spirit.

- I renew my mind to the truth of who God is and who I am:

    You are my loving, powerful Father, and I am your beloved child.

- I write down today's cares and worries:

_____

_____

_____

_____

_____

Are my worries realistic, Lord? Have I done my part to solve problems or help others solve them? Please show me.

I take each care, name it, and hand it to you. Here it is, Lord! By your grace, I will not worry about it anymore. I will keep my eyes on you and off my worries! Please strengthen me and walk with me now.

- I rejoice and praise God, and I thank him for my many blessings. These are things I am grateful for today:

_____

_____

_____

I praise you, Lord, because you are worthy of all praise!

- I stay in the light, being hopeful, taking my thoughts captive. I dwell on whatever is true, honorable, just, pure, lovely, gracious, excellent, and praiseworthy. When I am tempted to think anxious thoughts, I think about these things instead:

_____

_____

_____

Guide my thinking today, Lord.

- I am geared up! I have put on the full armor of God. I will, by God's grace, courageously stand firm and turn from worry to wonder today!

  Lord, I trust you and I love you above all things. I know that you will protect me today and give me all that I need. I thank you and I praise you.

All battles are first won or lost in the mind.

–attributed to St. Joan of Arc

Have no anxiety about anything, but in everything by prayer and supplication with thanksgiving let your requests be made known to God.

–Philippians 4:6

DAY 33   **DATE:** _____

- I offer myself to God:

    Here I am, Lord. Please fill me with your Spirit.

- I renew my mind to the truth of who God is and who I am:

    You are my loving, powerful Father, and I am your beloved child.

- I write down today's cares and worries:

_____

_____

_____

_____

_____

Are my worries realistic, Lord? Have I done my part to solve problems or help others solve them? Please show me.

I take each care, name it, and hand it to you. Here it is, Lord! By your grace, I will not worry about it anymore. I will keep my eyes on you and off my worries! Please strengthen me and walk with me now.

- I rejoice and praise God, and I thank him for my many blessings. These are things I am grateful for today:

_____

_____

_____

_____

I praise you, Lord, because you are worthy of all praise!

- I stay in the light, being hopeful, taking my thoughts captive. I dwell on whatever is true, honorable, just, pure, lovely, gracious, excellent, and praiseworthy. When I am tempted to think anxious thoughts, I think about these things instead:

_____

_____

_____

_____

Guide my thinking today, Lord.

- I am geared up! I have put on the full armor of God. I will, by God's grace, courageously stand firm and turn from worry to wonder today!

    Lord, I trust you and I love you above all things. I know that you will protect me today and give me all that I need. I thank you and I praise you.

All battles are first won or lost in the mind.

–attributed to St. Joan of Arc

Have no anxiety about anything, but in everything by prayer and supplication with thanksgiving let your requests be made known to God.

–Philippians 4:6

DAY 34   **DATE:** _____

- I offer myself to God:

    Here I am, Lord. Please fill me with your Spirit.

- I renew my mind to the truth of who God is and who I am:

    You are my loving, powerful Father, and I am your beloved child.

- I write down today's cares and worries:

_____

_____

_____

_____

_____

Are my worries realistic, Lord? Have I done my part to solve problems or help others solve them? Please show me.

I take each care, name it, and hand it to you. Here it is, Lord! By your grace, I will not worry about it anymore. I will keep my eyes on you and off my worries! Please strengthen me and walk with me now.

- I rejoice and praise God, and I thank him for my many blessings. These are things I am grateful for today:

_____

_____

_____

_____

I praise you, Lord, because you are worthy of all praise!

- I stay in the light, being hopeful, taking my thoughts captive. I dwell on whatever is true, honorable, just, pure, lovely, gracious, excellent, and praiseworthy. When I am tempted to think anxious thoughts, I think about these things instead:

_____

_____

_____

_____

Guide my thinking today, Lord.

- I am geared up! I have put on the full armor of God. I will, by God's grace, courageously stand firm and turn from worry to wonder today!

  Lord, I trust you and I love you above all things. I know that you will protect me today and give me all that I need. I thank you and I praise you.

All battles are first won or lost in the mind.

–attributed to St. Joan of Arc

Have no anxiety about anything, but in everything by prayer and supplication with thanksgiving let your requests be made known to God.

–Philippians 4:6

DAY 35   **DATE:** _____

- I offer myself to God:

    Here I am, Lord. Please fill me with your Spirit.

- I renew my mind to the truth of who God is and who I am:

    You are my loving, powerful Father, and I am your beloved child.

- I write down today's cares and worries:

_____

_____

_____

_____

_____

Are my worries realistic, Lord? Have I done my part to solve problems or help others solve them? Please show me.

I take each care, name it, and hand it to you. Here it is, Lord! By your grace, I will not worry about it anymore. I will keep my eyes on you and off my worries! Please strengthen me and walk with me now.

- I rejoice and praise God, and I thank him for my many blessings. These are things I am grateful for today:

_____

_____

_____

_____

I praise you, Lord, because you are worthy of all praise!

- I stay in the light, being hopeful, taking my thoughts captive. I dwell on whatever is true, honorable, just, pure, lovely, gracious, excellent, and praiseworthy. When I am tempted to think anxious thoughts, I think about these things instead:

_____

_____

_____

_____

Guide my thinking today, Lord.

- I am geared up! I have put on the full armor of God. I will, by God's grace, courageously stand firm and turn from worry to wonder today!

  Lord, I trust you and I love you above all things. I know that you will protect me today and give me all that I need. I thank you and I praise you.

All battles are first won or lost in the mind.

–attributed to St. Joan of Arc

Have no anxiety about anything, but in everything by prayer and supplication with thanksgiving let your requests be made known to God.

–Philippians 4:6

DAY 36   **DATE:** _____

- I offer myself to God:

    Here I am, Lord. Please fill me with your Spirit.

- I renew my mind to the truth of who God is and who I am:

    You are my loving, powerful Father, and I am your beloved child.

- I write down today's cares and worries:

_____

_____

_____

_____

_____

Are my worries realistic, Lord? Have I done my part to solve problems or help others solve them? Please show me.

I take each care, name it, and hand it to you. Here it is, Lord! By your grace, I will not worry about it anymore. I will keep my eyes on you and off my worries! Please strengthen me and walk with me now.

- I rejoice and praise God, and I thank him for my many blessings.
  These are things I am grateful for today:

_____

_____

_____

_____

I praise you, Lord, because you are worthy of all praise!

- I stay in the light, being hopeful, taking my thoughts captive.
  I dwell on whatever is true, honorable, just, pure, lovely, gracious,
  excellent, and praiseworthy. When I am tempted to think anxious
  thoughts, I think about these things instead:

_____

_____

_____

_____

Guide my thinking today, Lord.

- I am geared up! I have put on the full armor of God. I will, by
  God's grace, courageously stand firm and turn from worry to
  wonder today!

  *Lord, I trust you and I love you above all things. I know
  that you will protect me today and give me all that I need.
  I thank you and I praise you.*

All battles are first won or lost in the mind.

–attributed to St. Joan of Arc

Have no anxiety about anything, but in everything by prayer and supplication with thanksgiving let your requests be made known to God.

–Philippians 4:6

DAY 37   **DATE:** _____

- I offer myself to God:

    Here I am, Lord. Please fill me with your Spirit.

- I renew my mind to the truth of who God is and who I am:

    You are my loving, powerful Father, and I am your beloved child.

- I write down today's cares and worries:

_____

_____

_____

_____

_____

Are my worries realistic, Lord? Have I done my part to solve problems or help others solve them? Please show me.

I take each care, name it, and hand it to you. Here it is, Lord! By your grace, I will not worry about it anymore. I will keep my eyes on you and off my worries! Please strengthen me and walk with me now.

- I rejoice and praise God, and I thank him for my many blessings. These are things I am grateful for today:

_____

_____

_____

_____

I praise you, Lord, because you are worthy of all praise!

- I stay in the light, being hopeful, taking my thoughts captive. I dwell on whatever is true, honorable, just, pure, lovely, gracious, excellent, and praiseworthy. When I am tempted to think anxious thoughts, I think about these things instead:

_____

_____

_____

_____

Guide my thinking today, Lord.

- I am geared up! I have put on the full armor of God. I will, by God's grace, courageously stand firm and turn from worry to wonder today!

  Lord, I trust you and I love you above all things. I know that you will protect me today and give me all that I need. I thank you and I praise you.

All battles are first won or lost in the mind.

–attributed to St. Joan of Arc

Have no anxiety about anything, but in everything by prayer and supplication with thanksgiving let your requests be made known to God.

–Philippians 4:6

DAY 38 **DATE:** _____

- I offer myself to God:

    Here I am, Lord. Please fill me with your Spirit.

- I renew my mind to the truth of who God is and who I am:

    You are my loving, powerful Father, and I am your beloved child.

- I write down today's cares and worries:

_____

_____

_____

_____

_____

Are my worries realistic, Lord? Have I done my part to solve problems or help others solve them? Please show me.

I take each care, name it, and hand it to you. Here it is, Lord! By your grace, I will not worry about it anymore. I will keep my eyes on you and off my worries! Please strengthen me and walk with me now.

- I rejoice and praise God, and I thank him for my many blessings. These are things I am grateful for today:

I praise you, Lord, because you are worthy of all praise!

- I stay in the light, being hopeful, taking my thoughts captive. I dwell on whatever is true, honorable, just, pure, lovely, gracious, excellent, and praiseworthy. When I am tempted to think anxious thoughts, I think about these things instead:

Guide my thinking today, Lord.

- I am geared up! I have put on the full armor of God. I will, by God's grace, courageously stand firm and turn from worry to wonder today!

  Lord, I trust you and I love you above all things. I know that you will protect me today and give me all that I need. I thank you and I praise you.

All battles are first won or lost in the mind.

–attributed to St. Joan of Arc

Have no anxiety about anything, but in everything by prayer and supplication with thanksgiving let your requests be made known to God.

–Philippians 4:6

DAY 39   **DATE:** _____

- I offer myself to God:

    Here I am, Lord. Please fill me with your Spirit.

- I renew my mind to the truth of who God is and who I am:

    You are my loving, powerful Father, and I am your beloved child.

- I write down today's cares and worries:

_____

_____

_____

_____

_____

Are my worries realistic, Lord? Have I done my part to solve problems or help others solve them? Please show me.

I take each care, name it, and hand it to you. Here it is, Lord! By your grace, I will not worry about it anymore. I will keep my eyes on you and off my worries! Please strengthen me and walk with me now.

- I rejoice and praise God, and I thank him for my many blessings. These are things I am grateful for today:

_____

_____

_____

_____

I praise you, Lord, because you are worthy of all praise!

- I stay in the light, being hopeful, taking my thoughts captive. I dwell on whatever is true, honorable, just, pure, lovely, gracious, excellent, and praiseworthy. When I am tempted to think anxious thoughts, I think about these things instead:

_____

_____

_____

_____

Guide my thinking today, Lord.

- I am geared up! I have put on the full armor of God. I will, by God's grace, courageously stand firm and turn from worry to wonder today!

  Lord, I trust you and I love you above all things. I know that you will protect me today and give me all that I need. I thank you and I praise you.

All battles are first won or lost in the mind.

–attributed to St. Joan of Arc

Have no anxiety about anything, but in everything by prayer and supplication with thanksgiving let your requests be made known to God.

–Philippians 4:6

DAY 40   **DATE:** _____

- I offer myself to God:

    Here I am, Lord. Please fill me with your Spirit.

- I renew my mind to the truth of who God is and who I am:

    You are my loving, powerful Father, and I am your beloved child.

- I write down today's cares and worries:

_____

_____

_____

_____

_____

Are my worries realistic, Lord? Have I done my part to solve problems or help others solve them? Please show me.

I take each care, name it, and hand it to you. Here it is, Lord! By your grace, I will not worry about it anymore. I will keep my eyes on you and off my worries! Please strengthen me and walk with me now.

- I rejoice and praise God, and I thank him for my many blessings. These are things I am grateful for today:

_____

_____

_____

_____

I praise you, Lord, because you are worthy of all praise!

- I stay in the light, being hopeful, taking my thoughts captive. I dwell on whatever is true, honorable, just, pure, lovely, gracious, excellent, and praiseworthy. When I am tempted to think anxious thoughts, I think about these things instead:

_____

_____

_____

_____

Guide my thinking today, Lord.

- I am geared up! I have put on the full armor of God. I will, by God's grace, courageously stand firm and turn from worry to wonder today!

  Lord, I trust you and I love you above all things. I know that you will protect me today and give me all that I need. I thank you and I praise you.

All battles are first won or lost in the mind.

–attributed to St. Joan of Arc

A CLOSING NOTE

In the introduction, I told the story of my daughter's terrible accident. Along with the love of family and friends, there were three powerful spiritual practices that pulled us through those dark days:

- The promises in Sacred Scripture that I learned and claimed daily

- Christ's powerful presence in the sacrament of the Eucharist

- The sustaining support I felt through prayer to the Blessed Mother in the Rosary

God gives us his grace in so many forms, most powerfully in the gift of himself.

To get the most out of the tools we have explored here—to gain the power to change—I recommend that you go to confession, attend daily Mass, and pray the Rosary every day. Then pray through the Scriptures and promises found in this book, casting your cares upon him—if you can, in a church where he abides in the tabernacle or in an Adoration chapel. There is nothing more life-giving than choosing to meet in person with the Author of life himself and receiving him, Body and Blood, Soul and Divinity, in the Eucharist. Try this and see how our loving Lord blesses you tremendously as you seek him in this way.

And remember, the Blessed Mother is always close by to lend a hand. If it is not already a part of your prayer practice, the Rosary is another little stick of dynamite, and you can keep the beads in your pocket. You can also keep them in your hand or under your pillow when you sleep and give them a squeeze if you wake during the night. Pray a decade as you wait for sleep to return. Picture all the Rosary prayers that have ever been prayed going straight up to heaven and the Blessed Mother wrapping you in her mantle of love. Ask for God's peace to flow over you and keep you safe and secure as you sleep. A friend of mine calls this "the rosary clutch," and it works! The Rosary is our direct connection to the Blessed Mother, who never leaves unaided anyone who seeks her help.[17]

These are the tools that the Church has given us: Sacred Scripture and Sacred Tradition; Christ present in the sacraments, especially the Holy Eucharist, where he is physically present; and the Blessed Mother. Prayer and the sacraments are the awesome, supernatural weapons we possess to combat worry and find our rest and peace in God.

PART III

A WORRY-TO-WONDER TOOLKIT

A Worry-to-Wonder Checklist to Go

Talk-Back Truths

Prayers and Hymns

Recommended Reading

Here is an at-a-glance checklist to remind you of God's promises throughout the day. You can cut it out and, if you like, laminate or frame it. If you are like me, you will want to keep the list on hand to remind you of God's truth in his holy Word.

A WORRY-TO-WONDER CHECKLIST TO GO

☐ **Refresh your spirit:** Offer yourself to the Lord every morning.

"Present your bodies as a living sacrifice, holy and acceptable to God." (Romans 12:1)

☐ **Plug into the power source:** Know who God is and what he can do.

"Be transformed by the renewal of your mind." (Romans 12:2)

☐ **Get understanding:** Know who you are and what you can do.

"I can do all things in him who strengthens me." (Philippians 4:13)

☐ **Be set free:** Cast your cares on the Lord.

"Cast all your anxieties on him, for he cares about you." (1 Peter 5:7)

☐ **Look up!** Rejoice and be grateful.

"Rejoice in the Lord always ... Have no anxiety about anything." (Philippians 4:4, 6)

☐ **Stay in the light:** Guide your thoughts to what is good.

"If there is any excellence, if there is anything worthy of praise, think about these things." (Philippians 4:8)

☐ **Act in God's strength:** Courageously stand firm.

"Be strong in the Lord and in the strength of his might. Put on the whole armor of God." (Ephesians 6:10-11)

TALK-BACK TRUTHS

When you are tempted to worry, remind yourself in whom you place your trust and what he can do—and be transformed!

When the Enemy says:	You reply:	Scripture
"God is holding out on you. If he were truly good, a God of love, you would not be in this situation."	"God is love and nothing can separate me from his love."	Romans 8:38-39
"You are all done!"	"I trust in God! And there is nothing too difficult for him."	Jeremiah 32:27
"There is no hope! It is over! Walk away!"	"I trust in a good, creator God who makes all things new, again and again! I can begin again!"	Revelation 21:5
"You are all alone. God has forgotten about you."	"My God will never fail me; never will he forsake me. In that I place my trust!"	Deuteronomy 31:8
"Who do you think you are? You are just a sinner, a failure, not a saint!"	"I am God's beloved child. And by his grace, I am chosen, redeemed, and capable of holiness and victory!"	Isaiah 43:1
"Your trials are too much for you. Give in!"	"I have faith in God, who will deliver me!"	1 Corinthians 10:13
"You are all alone. Give up!"	"I am strong because God is always with me!"	Joshua 1:9
"You are weak and cowardly!"	"By his Spirit, I am brave, powerful, and full of self-control!"	2 Timothy 1:7
"You have not got enough. You are *not* going to make it!"	"God is with me. I am not afraid. I *can* do this!"	Psalm 118:6
"You can't do it!"	"I can do all things through him who gives me strength!"	Philippians 4:13
"You are not enough."	(Agree!) "But my strength is in Jesus. In God's unlimited strength, I am capable of victory!"	Psalm 18:1-2

PRAYERS AND HYMNS

The Rosary

Begin by making the Sign of the Cross and kissing your rosary. Say the Apostles' Creed (while holding the crucifix of your rosary). Pray one Our Father (first bead), three Hail Marys (second, third, and fourth beads), and one Glory Be (fifth bead). Announce the first mystery and pray one Our Father. Pray ten Hail Marys on the next "decade" (ten beads), meditating on the mystery, and end with one Glory Be and the Fatima Prayer. On the next bead, announce the second mystery, and repeat the steps until you have prayed all five decades. Close with the Hail, Holy Queen and the Rosary prayer.

PRAYERS IN THE ROSARY

The Apostles' Creed

I believe in God, the Father almighty, Creator of heaven and earth, and in Jesus Christ, his only Son, our Lord, who was conceived by the Holy Spirit, born of the Virgin Mary, suffered under Pontius Pilate, was crucified, died and was buried; he descended to hell; on the third day he rose again from the dead; he ascended into heaven, and is seated at the right hand of God the Father almighty; from there he will come to judge the living and the dead. I believe in the Holy Spirit, the holy catholic Church, the communion of saints, the forgiveness of sins, the resurrection of the body, and life everlasting. Amen.

Our Father

Our Father, who art in heaven, hallowed be thy name; thy kingdom come, thy will be done, on earth as it is in heaven. Give us this day our daily bread; and forgive us our trespasses as we forgive those who trespass against us; and lead us not into temptation; but deliver us from evil. Amen.

Hail Mary

Hail Mary, full of grace, the Lord is with thee. Blessed art thou among women, and blessed is the fruit of thy womb, Jesus. Holy Mary, Mother of God, pray for us sinners, now and at the hour of our death. Amen.

Glory Be

Glory be to the Father, and to the Son, and to the Holy Spirit, as it was in the beginning, is now, and ever shall be, world without end. Amen.

Fatima Prayer

O my Jesus, forgive us our sins, save us from the fires of hell, and lead all souls to heaven, especially those in most need of thy mercy.

Hail, Holy Queen

Hail, Holy Queen, Mother of mercy, our life, our sweetness, and our hope. To thee do we cry, poor banished children of Eve; to thee do we send up our sighs, mourning and weeping in this valley of tears. Turn, then, most gracious advocate, thine eyes of mercy toward us, and after this our exile, show unto us the blessed fruit of thy womb, Jesus. O clement, O loving, O sweet Virgin Mary.

Pray for us, O holy Mother of God.

That we may be made worthy of the promises of Christ.

Rosary Prayer

Let us pray: O God, whose only begotten Son, by his life, death, and resurrection, has purchased for us the rewards of eternal life, grant, we beseech thee, that meditating upon these mysteries of the Most Holy Rosary of the Blessed Virgin Mary, we may imitate what they contain and obtain what they promise, through the same Christ our Lord. Amen.

THE MYSTERIES OF THE ROSARY

Glorious Mysteries (Sunday and Wednesday)

1. The Resurrection
2. The Ascension
3. The Descent of the Holy Spirit
4. The Assumption of Mary
5. The Coronation of Mary

Joyful Mysteries (Monday and Saturday)

1. The Annunciation
2. The Visitation
3. The Nativity
4. The Presentation
5. The Finding of Jesus in the Temple

Sorrowful Mysteries (Tuesday and Friday)

1. The Agony in the Garden
2. The Scourging at the Pillar
3. The Crowning with Thorns
4. The Carrying of the Cross
5. The Crucifixion

Luminous Mysteries (Thursday)

1. The Baptism of Jesus
2. The Wedding at Cana
3. The Proclamation of the Kingdom
4. The Transfiguration
5. The Institution of the Eucharist

Memorare

Remember, O most gracious Virgin Mary, that never was it known that anyone who fled to thy protection, implored thy help, or sought thy intercession was left unaided. Inspired with this confidence, I fly unto thee, O Virgin of virgins, my Mother; to thee do I come, before thee I stand, sinful and sorrowful. O Mother of the Word Incarnate, despise not my petitions, but in thy mercy, hear and answer me. Amen.

The *Te Deum*

> *Bless the LORD, O my soul; and all that is within me,*
> *bless his holy name!*
>
> –Psalm 103:1

The *Te Deum* is an ancient Latin hymn sung in the Liturgy of the Hours on most Sundays and other days of rejoicing. Its full Latin title, *Te Deum laudamus*, means "God, we praise you."

You are God: we praise you;
You are God: we acclaim you;
You are the eternal Father:
All creation worships you.
To you all angels, all the powers of heaven,
Cherubim and Seraphim, sing in endless praise:
Holy, holy, holy, Lord, God of power and might,
Heaven and earth are full of your glory.
The glorious company of apostles praise you.
The noble fellowship of prophets praise you.
The white-robed army of martyrs praise you.
Throughout the world the holy Church acclaims you:
Father, of majesty unbounded,
Your true and only Son, worthy of all worship,

And the Holy Spirit, advocate and guide.
You, Christ, are the king of glory,
The eternal Son of the Father.
When you became man to set us free
You did not spurn the Virgin's womb.
You overcame the sting of death,
And opened the kingdom of heaven to all believers.
You are seated at God's right hand in glory.
We believe that you will come, and be our judge.
Come then, Lord, and help your people,
Bought with the price of your own blood,
And bring us with your saints
To glory everlasting.
Save your people, Lord, and bless your inheritance.
Govern and uphold them now and always.
Day by day we bless you.
We praise your name forever.
Keep us today, Lord, from all sin.
Have mercy on us, Lord, have mercy.
Lord, show us your love and mercy;
For we put our trust in you.
In you, Lord, is our hope:
And we shall never hope in vain.[18]

Hymn Lyrics

These are a few of my favorite hymns that I carry in my heart. I share them here to help you cast your glance upward and behold His Majesty.

"Immortal, Invisible, God Only Wise"

by Walter C. Smith (1867)

1. Immortal, invisible, God only wise,
   in light inaccessible, hid from our eyes,
   most blessed, most glorious, the Ancient of Days,
   almighty, victorious, thy great name we praise.

2. Unresting, unhasting, and silent as light,
   nor wanting, nor wasting, thou rulest in might,
   thy justice like mountains high soaring above
   thy clouds, which are fountains of goodness and love.

3. To all, life thou givest, to both great and
   small. In all life thou livest, the true life of all.
   We blossom and flourish as leaves on the tree,
   and wither and perish, but naught changeth thee.

4. Great God of all glory, great God of all light,
   thine angels adore thee, all veiling their sight.
   All praise we would render; O help us to see
   'tis only the splendor of light hideth thee.[19]

"Let All Mortal Flesh Keep Silence"

from the Liturgy of St. James, paraphrased by Gerard Moultrie (1864)

1. Let all mortal flesh keep silence,
    and with fear and trembling stand.
    Ponder nothing earthly minded,
    for with blessing in his hand
    Christ our God to earth descending
    comes, our homage to demand.

2. King of kings, yet born of Mary,
    as of old on earth he stood,
    Lord of heaven now incarnate
    in the body and the blood,
    he will give to all the faithful
    his own self for heav'nly food.

3. Rank on rank the host of heaven
    streams before him on the way,
    as the Light of light descending
    from the realms of endless day
    comes, that pow'rs of hell may vanish,
    as the shadows pass away.

4. At his feet the six-winged seraph,
    cherubim with sleepless eye,
    veil their faces to the Presence
    as with ceaseless voice they cry,
    "Alleluia! Alleluia!
    Alleluia, Lord Most High!"[20]

"Holy, Holy, Holy! Lord God Almighty!"

by Reginald Heber (1826)

1. Holy, holy, holy! Lord God almighty!
   Early in the morning our song shall rise to thee.
   Holy, holy, holy! Merciful and mighty!
   God in three persons, blessed trinity!

2. Holy, holy, holy! All the saints adore thee,
   casting down their golden crowns around the glassy sea;
   cherubim and seraphim falling down before thee,
   which wert, and art, and evermore shalt be.

3. Holy, holy, holy! Though the darkness hide thee,
   though the eye of sinfulness thy glory may not see,
   only thou art holy; there is none beside thee,
   perfect in pow'r, in love, and purity.

4. Holy, holy, holy! Lord God almighty!
   All thy works shall praise thy name, in earth, and sky, and sea.
   Holy, holy, holy! Merciful and mighty!
   God in three persons, blessed trinity![21]

RECOMMENDED READING

Athanasius, Jerome, Sulpicius Severus, and Gregory the Great. *Early Christian Lives*. Edited and translated by Carolinne White. New York: Penguin Books, 1998.

Evagrius of Pontus. *Talking Back: A Monastic Handbook for Combating Demons*. Translated by David Brakke. Cistercian Studies Series, no. 229. Collegeville, MN: Liturgical Press, 2009.

Philippe, Jacques. *In the School of the Holy Spirit*. Translated by Helena Scott. New York: Scepter, 2007.

Philippe, Jacques. *Interior Freedom*. Translated by Helena Scott. New York: Scepter, 2007.

Pivonka, Dave. *Breath of God: Living a Life Led by the Holy Spirit*. Notre Dame, IN: Ave Maria Press, 2015.

Stinissen, Wilfrid. *Into Your Hands, Father: Abandoning Ourselves to the God Who Loves Us*. Translated by Sr. Clare Marie. San Francisco: Ignatius, 2011.

Ward, Benedicta, trans. *The Desert Fathers: Sayings of the Early Christian Monks*. New York: Penguin Books, 2003.

ACKNOWLEDGMENTS

I would like to thank God, first and foremost, for writing the best parts of this book—the Holy Scriptures, the sure foundation on which all else is built—and for giving me the honor of serving him in this way. I would like to thank Rebecca Robinson for her immeasurable help and many hours of hard work editing this book and encouraging me "not to worry" along the way—and all of the wonderful people at Ascension, especially Jeff Cavins, Matt Pinto, Meredith Wilson, and the team who helped bring this book to life. And thanks to my professors at the Augustine Institute, especially Dr. John Sehorn for introducing me to the Church Fathers, all of whom have inspired me and taught me so much about faith and trust in God. I also want to thank my dear friends Maribeth Harper, who helped me originally organize my thoughts and get them onto paper; Dr. Anita Gadhia-Smith, who encouragingly said this book would be helpful to many; and all of my friends and family who were patient with me and suffered through the writing process, especially Dale and Daisy! And last, I want to thank Fr. Zachary Dominguez, who believed in me and helped equip me to live courageously free; Fr. Stephen Ellis, who helps me keep going from "worry to wonder" each day; and Fr. John Paul Pietropaoli, who always guides my writing to "correctness." God bless you all, and thank you. May God be praised.

NOTES

1. See Exodus 15:11 and Romans 8:28.

2. For the context of this quote, see "Man Fully Alive Is the Glory of God – Irenaeus," Crossroads Initiative, June 20, 2021, crossroadsinitiative.com.

3. Thérèse of Lisieux, "Abandonment Is the Sweet Fruit of Love," in *The Poetry of Saint Thérèse of Lisieux*, trans. Donald Kinney (Washington, DC: ICS Publications, 2020), verse 7. This poem is dated May 31, 1897.

4. Thérèse of Lisieux, *The Story of a Soul: The Autobiography of The Little Flower*, trans. Michael Day (Charlotte, NC: TAN Classics, 2010), chap. 9, books.google.com.

5. Thérèse of Lisieux, chap. 9.

6. "Homily of His Holiness John Paul II for the Inauguration of His Pontificate" (October 22, 1978), 5, vatican.va.

7. The "Prayer of Self-Offering" is reprinted here by the kind permission of the author, Peter Bond, of CatholicPrayerCards.org.

8. Abraham Lincoln, as cited by Donald G. Barnhouse, *God's River, Romans 5:1-11* (Grand Rapids: Eerdmans, 1958), 39, quoted in Alan F. Johnson, "The New Situation: Freedom from the Wrath of God; 5:1-21," in *Romans*, Everyman's Bible Commentary (Chicago: Moody, 2000), books.google.com.

9. Rick Warren, *The Purpose Driven Life* (Grand Rapids, MI: Zondervan, 2012), 262.

10. Teresa of Avila, *Interior Castle*, ed. and trans. E. Allison Peers (Mineola, NY: Dover, 2007), 24.

11. Jacques Philippe, *Interior Freedom*, trans. Helena Scott (New York: Scepter, 2007), 86–87.

12. Bible Hub, s.v. "5463. chairó," accessed September 3, 2021, biblehub.com.

13. Bible Hub, s.v. "1451. eggus," accessed September 3, 2021, biblehub.com.

14. Bible Hub, s.v. "3309. merimnaó," accessed September 3, 2021, biblehub.com.

15. Thomist theologian Reginald Garrigou-Lagrange (quoted in Louis Bouyer, *The Spirit and Forms of Protestantism*, trans. A.V. Littledale [Princeton, NJ: Scepter, 2001], 73) summarized the Catholic position when he observed that "in the work of salvation *all is from God*, including our own cooperation, in the sense that we cannot distinguish *a part as exclusively ours* that does not come from the author of all good."

16. Athanasius, "Life of Antony," in *Early Christian Lives*, ed. and trans. Carolinne White (New York: Penguin Books, 1998), 13.

17. Instructions for praying the Rosary appear in Part III of the book.

18. *Compendium of the Catechism of the Catholic Church* (Libreria Editrice Vaticana, 2005), vatican.va.

19. Walter C. Smith, "Immortal, Invisible, God Only Wise," Hymnary.org, accessed August 30, 2021, hymnary.org.

20. Gerard Moultrie, "Let All Mortal Flesh Keep Silence," Hymnary.org, accessed August 30, 2021, hymnary.org.

21. Reginald Heber, "Holy, Holy, Holy! Lord God Almighty!," Hymnary.org, accessed September 3, 2021, hymnary.org.